S0-EAZ-123

SISTERS *of* MARYKNOLL

SISTERS *of* MARYKNOLL

Through Troubled Waters

By

Sister Mary de Paul Cogan

Essay Index Reprint Series

BOOKS FOR LIBRARIES PRESS
FREEPORT, NEW YORK

Nihil obstat

JOHN M. A. FEARNS, S.T.D.
CENSOR LIBRORUM.

Imprimatur

✠ FRANCIS CARDINAL SPELLMAN,
ARCHBISHOP OF NEW YORK

Library of Congress Cataloging in Publication Data

Cogan, Mary de Paul, Sister.
Sisters of Maryknoll through troubled waters.

(Essay index reprint series)
1. Maryknoll Sisters of St. Dominic. I. Title.
[BV2300.M4C64 1972] 266'.2 72-167329
ISBN 0-8369-2764-8

PRINTED IN THE UNITED STATES OF AMERICA
BY
NEW WORLD BOOK MANUFACTURING CO., INC.
HALLANDALE, FLORIDA 33009

Preface

A FEW frightened fishermen crouching in an upper room in Jerusalem . . . "And there appeared to them parted tongues as it were of fire, and it sat upon every one of them." In the twinkling of an eye had begun the fierce and tumultuous struggle which was to cast forth that fire into the uttermost corners of the globe. That very day were added to the Catholic Church three thousand souls. That very day started the great missionary "trek" which has wound its way all around the globe. The casting of that fire has been a work hot and arduous. Full of struggle and strain and defeat; full of failures and new beginnings. But it has been a pageant full of life and brilliance and glory—of color and movement. The forward missionary surge of the Catholic Church catches up in every age the richest contributions of chosen souls and carries them along in its eager march.

Eager were the first missionary bishops who travelled to Greece, Rome, Spain and Africa. Eager were the neophytes whom they left behind, hiding in obscure corners of a hostile pagan world. And just as eager and of kindred spirit were the missioners of yesterday found by America's fighting men on every front in the war of the Pacific.

The conflagration is over but the interest in the innate nobility of mind and soul as it faces the tragic realities and the dramatic commonplaces of war courageously and with a saving sense of humor never ends. Admiration deepens for the undaunted spirit that with peace begins, in alien lands, a rebuilding amidst catastrophic destruction. There is a public of readers avid for accounts of war experiences and reconstruction efforts.

These brief, blunt reports from Maryknoll Sisters, which tell how they carried on in the Orient when war brought their missionary activities to a standstill, relate a story of devotion to God and man, ever old and ever new. These heroic missioners make no pretense to heroism. In refugee colonies, in Japanese concentration camps, they turned to tasks nearest at hand. With the American forces they served as nurses, as trained secretaries; Sister doctors cared for the army of the dispossessed, and other

Sisters helped feed the starving hordes; interned, the Sisters nursed and taught and cooked and sewed, played with the children and helped sustain the morale of the elders. Their experiences they relate directly, simply, forcibly, without attempt at literary elaboration. The very impact of the raw facts leaves the thoughtful reader profoundly shaken and humbled.

In these reports we see a new example of the exaltation of the human spirit which comes to great souls when they face great dangers; when fortitude is forged in the crucible of suffering; when the charity of Christ presses the soul of the missionary to consummate its sacrifice in martyrdom. With humility and envy we watch the Maryknollers carry the spirit of their vocation into their unchosen war-time service. Theirs is a healthy, well-balanced spirit, full of holiness and humor; a spirit that can make light of a thousand mile journey in sampan, river-boat, Chinese truck and bus, American jeep and decrepit train; a spirit that can emphasize homely, human incidents in the midst of cities blazing with bomb-fire, camps frightful with famine, jails shorn of all privacy, shrapnel-sprayed hillside and espionage close and constant, designed to wreck minds and conquer souls.

When the glow of these great and dangerous days has faded somewhat, this book will stand as a reminder of the priceless legacy of missionary greatness. It is the greatness which Christ taught on the Cross. "Unless the grain of wheat falling into the ground die, itself remaineth alone. But if it die, it bringeth forth much fruit." Maryknoll had no fear that the seed of faith planted in the Orient would not be harvested. Though its houses were leveled to the ground, its personnel scattered to the four winds, its works interrupted, native priests, native Sisters and native Christians, trained and developed by these selfless missionaries, were jealously guarding the treasure, and some day Maryknoll would return.

That day has come. Departure ceremonies bid Godspeed to the occupational army of Christ, in whose heart flames the fire of Love. Friends of Maryknoll since its inception, and new friends to be made through this simple narrative for America's first Catholic missionary foundation, join in prayers and good wishes for a bright future.

✠Richard J. Cushing
Archbishop of Boston

Contents

SISTERS
of
MARYKNOLL

PART ONE

The Philippines

1

Fine Tempered Steel

THE story begins in the refugee-strewn corridors of Muntinlupa Prison when the hearty voice of Lt. Com. Jordan echoed through the concrete, heavily barred cells, "Where are the Sisters who want to go home?"

It rose to a climax in the old parish church of San Bartolome, Malabon, badly in need of repair but still majestic in line, when priest and people chanted a solemn Te Deum after the Sunday Mass.

It is the story of the Maryknoll Sisters' return to their work interrupted but fructified by three and a half years of internment and the inevitable hardships of war.

We had been taken to Muntinlupa Prison on February 23, 1945, after our rescue from the Los Baños Internment Camp. There, through the kindness of the American Army, we ate and rested for nearly two months, putting pound after pound on the spare frames the internment camp had left us.

They were restless months, however. We were anxious to return to our missions—to open our schools, to live with the Filipino people, to do the work God sent us here to do. So when, on a Saturday, Lt. Com. Jordan of the United States Navy offered to take us three Sisters home to Malabon the following Tuesday, we accepted on the dot.

It took about half an hour after Mass to pack our goods and chattels into a couple of cardboard cartons and *tampipis,* native boxes woven of buri palm. Then we sat beside our prison bunks looking as if we were waiting for the Golden Chariot to take us across the River Jordan. Well, we only hoped the charioteer would not forget his promise.

He didn't, although he was so late we almost gave up hope. "Where are those Sisters who said they wanted to go home?

Are they ready yet?" His voice rang along the corridor joyously.

"Here we are, here we are!" Ready? Why, we had been ready to go "home" ever since Christmas Day, 1941, when we had to leave it. So we went—packed snugly in the jeep with boxes and bags. The last thing to be brought out was a white enamel pail full of empty tin cans. Dr. Jordan held it up.

"Want this?" he asked.

Of course we wanted it! Just try to pry an ex-internee loose from good tin cans. Tin cans are cooking pots, plates and cups, bath tubs, pitchers, basins, strainers, bottles, colanders, rain catchers—everything an internee needs and hasn't. It took some firm insisting but we persuaded him at last to let us keep the cans. A good thing, too, for we are still cooking in them. Sister Maria del Rey was told to hold the cans tight to keep them from rattling louder than the jeep, and we started for Malabon. A wave to the Lucena Sisters, our St. Paul's Hospital Sisters, our Normal School and St. Mary's Hall Sisters—poor Sisters, their homes were but debris and ashes.

We stopped at a Sea Bee encampment in Las Piñas; the Chief Officer invited us to dinner. Imagine, eating with Sea Bees in a Quonset hut! Sea Bees are men *you* read about and admire from a distance; Quonset huts are things *you* see in the rotogravure section. But *we* stood in line with Sea Bees, carrying one of those big tin trays with food-compartments and a tin can for the cold drink. (Yes. We did need them!) It was the first time, the officer said, that women had eaten with that company. There was a sign at the front gate, Positively No Women, but the sentry had waved us through.

We fitted ourselves into the jeep again and went on through the ruins of Manila, stopping only long enough to look at the pile of rock and rubble that once was beautiful Assumption College, rich in the traditions of the best Philippine families. We had been interned there for two and one-half years during the early part of the Japanese occupation. It was a house of many grateful memories for gracious deeds.

War correspondents can describe Manila better than we. They are paid to look for appropriate adjectives. The narrow lanes through the shambles, which have been cleared for traffic are filled with army buses, army trucks, jeeps, ducks, tractors, bull-dozers, derricks. The size and equipment of this army is breath-taking; it has rolled over the Philippines like a kindly juggernaut.

The jeep bowled merrily along Rizal Extension—La Loma and the Chinese Cemeteries, Caloocan, Grace Park, turn left at the Monument, Sangandaan and the fish-ponds. Already we could see the two towers of San Bartolome Church above the nipa roofs, and the bulk of the old convento beside it. Home, still there and waiting for us!

The bridge leading into Malabon was blown out. We had to leave the jeep in the care of the Guevara family. "Nanay, nanay, come quick! The Sisters are back!" and ferry across the river in a dugout banca. The ferry-boy would not take the money; he used to bring children to our school in the old days. Sufficient for him that the Sisters had returned.

That was the beginning of the welcome which has not stopped yet—after a month. Several of our old pupils, now grown beyond recognition, perspired manfully under the luggage from the ferry to the convento. As we proceeded down the dusty street, beaming faces came to the windows and beckoned to other faces behind them. "Look, Sister, my youngest. Born during the war."

Fifteen minutes after the familiar doors had closed behind us, the news was all over town. The oldest and dearest friends came to shake hands all around three or four times, and to say about twenty times, "Very glad, very, very glad!" So many of them were in black. Brothers had been executed; husbands had been taken and not heard from; sons had died in combat or in guerrilla warfare. Our alumni roster has many gold stars, many heroes.

Our former teachers, those Adriano and Punzalan girls who were so faithful and so generous all through the war years—they were on hand of course, and thinking of the practical things. They got beds and set them up in the former refectory. They dug out plates and saucers from the dusty heaps in the store-rooms. They unearthed a clay stove and rigged up a cooking place on the back porch.

That was Tuesday, when the Malabon house was set up again with three Sisters—Sisters David Marie, Patricia Marie and Maria del Rey. The rest of the week for us was just a series of visits, seeing the old friends, meeting the new ones. No one came empty handed. Indeed, since we returned, we have lived entirely on charity. It is Siochi's bread, Adriano's meat, Santos' eggs, Father Ignacio's bananas, Amparo's lettuce and green peppers, that greet us when we sit down to dinner. And very often a dessert arrives just at the right time for it. We think with good reason that the neighbors have estimated very keenly our needs and there is a regular system for filling them.

The following Sunday, a High Mass of Thanksgiving for the Sisters' return, was sung in the parish church. The choir was composed of about ten young men who have formed a Sanctuary Club. To hear their rich young voices offering praise to God, to see their tall figures move so reverently around the altar—it was tremendous for us.

After the Mass, Father Ignacio, our little Filipino pastor, laid aside his vestments and donned the cope. We wondered. Benediction after Mass? No, it was the boys' big surprise. Father intoned, "Te Deum Laudamus!"; the choir took it up joyously, "Te Deum confitemur." The music rolled from the choir behind the screen, across the tiled sanctuary floor to where Father was incensing the altar, and back to us, standing in the old accustomed pew in the front of the congregation.

We were home, home to stay, among our people.

Sister Maria del Rey, formerly of Pittsburgh, once an embryonic newspaper woman, thus describes graphically the reopening of a Maryknoll mission outside Manila.

In the Far East, private or government transportation is non-existent so far as the lay population is concerned. "Going my way?" is a query current among service drivers. Priests and Sisters who left their stations just in advance of the invaders, by foot, cycle, river boat, refugee train, or as in the Philippines were moved to concentration camps under Japanese armed guards are returning by jeep and peep; in truck and on weapon carrier; aboard B 25's and L 5's, and their British counterparts.

Sister Monica Marie, R.N. with a small group of Sister nurses and assistants served in an American Army Hospital in Kunming, China. Sister writes under date of September 16, 1945:

Our old outfit, 95th Station Hospital, is breaking up and going home to America in a unit. They tell us we are part of their unit and should go with them; they cannot understand why we are so happy to be going home to our mission in the interior. . . . Some of my patients were shot down over our old territory, between Loking and Loting. It is a small world—smaller than ever now! . . . We'll be flown out in a few days. Only an L-5 can land on Taan Chuk as the field was destroyed practically, and there is but a narrow, repaired landing strip. It will be good to get back and see our poor people again. I'll have to polish up my Cantonese. Around here everyone speaks Mandarin.

In this war the band of missioners and the fighting forces forged close bonds—perhaps they are but serving in different branches in the Army of the Lord. The serviceman may not always understand the motive that draws a missioner to his distant post, but he recognizes the good work that is done, in many instances has profited by it, and he does all in his power to make the return possible and living easier. A letter from a Chaplain to Mother Mary Joseph, Foundress and Mother General of the Maryknoll Sisters, gives a picture of this mutual helpfulness. The Reverend Captain was with a Division in Baguio, after its liberation. He writes:

Shortly after we took Baguio I went into your convent to save any valuables that might be left. My surprise was great to discover that your Sisters had already returned, for until the caves were cleared out, the place was not safe. . . . The convent was not a pretty sight, as artillery shells damaged one side and the roof above the chapel was completely gone. Doors were torn away and windows just didn't exist; the place was dirty and enough had happened to make it a discouraging sight. But the Sisters were in good spirits, despite the hardships they had endured in the prison camps.

As soon as the men heard of their presence they wanted to help. They repaired the road, roofed the chapel, replaced the window frames and even located some panes of glass. They tried to provide food, and we managed to get a little clothing for them. . . .

I wish I could tell all the people back home of the great force for good the Sisters have exerted on our boys. It is not an exaggeration to say they were the greatest single influence on our men since they have been overseas. First, Maryknoll spelt HOME to the men. Believe me they even asked for passes to visit the Sisters! Your convent took on the aspect of a railway terminal and the turn-over was just about as fast. Officers and enlisted men, Catholic and Protestant alike, the rough, the gruff, the gentle, the shy. The coffee pot was always on the stove and the Sisters' hospitality was universally known. The fellows claimed it was the closest to home they had been since they left. . . .

The Convent is that—a happy home. The Sisters show visibly their love of God. That is why it is such a gathering place for everyone. They have done more good than any Padre could.

I believe our boys helped them also. The terrible change after their prison camps, the loss of one of their number in the evacuation of Baguio naturally would make for bad memories. Because the boys talked always about themselves, the Sisters had no time to think of the past. My artillery crowd took up a collection. The Sisters designated it for a chapel erected in honor of the Division and for the use of their poor Igorot people.

Two hundred and forty Maryknoll Sisters were stationed in the East as follows when on December 8, 1941, Pearl Harbor was attacked and a few hours later bombs fell on Baguio:

Hawaii	85
Philippines	53
Macao	2
South China	31
Hong Kong	26
Japan	4
Korea	12
Manchukuo	27
	240

Two other Sisters, Sister Sylvester and Sister Edwardine were on board the S.S. *Coolidge,* not long out of Manila Bay. Sister Sylvester was coming home to die—after close to two decades spent "amid the alien"—rice paddies of Korea. When in October the Sisters reluctantly left Korea for the long trek homeward, their route was by way of Shanghai and the Philippines. By radio they heard the declaration of a state of war, they listened to enemy accounts of the sinking of their ship, to reports of the loss of their companion ship. It was a thrill, some twenty hours before they finally reached Oahu to see the great hulk of a President vessel against the horizon. When the Coolidge stopped at Honolulu hundreds of the victims of the first attack were taken aboard to be brought back to the United States for medical care. From Hawaii to California, Sister Edwardine, a trained nurse, and two Maryknoll Fathers on their decennial leave, spent twenty hours a day in attendance on the suffering service men.

The Maryknoll Fathers have been in the Orient since 1918; the Sisters since 1921. The two groups, canonically erected as The Catholic Foreign Mission Society of America and The Foreign Mission Sisters of St. Dominic, one in aim, one in spirit, one in its loved title *Maryknoll,* are distinct organizations, ecclesiastically and financially. These foundations mark the passage of the Catholic Church in the United States from the status of a mission Church to that of a Church of missioners. There was not only a strong native clergy, but there was a sensitiveness to hear and the willingness to obey the apostolic command "go and teach" others.

Reverend James Anthony Walsh (later Bishop Walsh) was the pioneer in a work which reached out far beyond the great Pacific. Prophets said that American boys and girls reared in the comforts of the States could not stand the poverty of the hinterland of Asia; that the heat of the Tropics would break their health if not their spirit; that the cold of the North would work havoc with bodies tempered to steam heat, but the Boston priest and his confreres believed in the stamina of the youth of their country—nor was their faith betrayed. In 1911 a tiny Seminary of three students was founded at Hawthorne, in Westchester, New York. A year later the beginning of a Sisters community took shape under the direction of Father Walsh and the leadership of Mary Josephine Rogers—a Smith College graduate, a teacher and a science instructor at Smith. In 1912, the tiny seeds were transplanted to a site north of Ossining, on Sunset Hill overlooking the Hudson at one of its most expansive stretches. The large farm and the small cottages received the name of Maryknoll—a tribute to Our Lady, Mother of God, patroness of the societies, and descriptive of the new site. Three decades have passed. The Knoll is crowned by two large buildings, examples of fine architectural integrity—a massive gray stone structure with marked Chinese touches in its turned-up roof corners and in its red trim, the center house of the Maryknoll

Fathers, and the Sisters Motherhouse warm in its autumn tones of yellow and tan and brown brick, reminiscent of the old Spanish missions in its graceful arches, broad patio, and flowing fountain. The first young people trained on this hill top and sent over plain and mountain of the Far East have grown old in the service. They and their followers have endured heroically the sufferings of war; they face unflinchingly the apparent ruin of their life's work and ask only that to them may fall the privilege of helping in the reconstruction.

On the battle fronts of the Eastern world the tried missioner and the young soldier have stood—fine tempered steel both.

2

Epistles from the Philippines

Somewhere in the Philippines
February 25, 1945

Dearest Mother,

Greetings—again and again! We hope *you* are well, Mother, and the Sisters, everyone—down to the newest postulant! How we *feel* the union of prayer!

Not knowing who wrote, what was said—this goes. We are safe—thanks be to God! and to the liberating AIRBORNE that did the work! More details will follow as soon as possible.

Sister Trinita was released to us January 1, 1945, after nine months in Fort Santiago which has a reputation of the worst degree. That was a miracle! She has such an indomitable spirit that after only a month she is much less the returned *ghost!* Sister Brigida was in, too; brave soul. We are expecting her here from the Philippine General Hospital via Santo Tomas Internment Camp. Sister de Chantal carried on beautifully in Sister Trinita's absence. Sister Rose Matthew suffered much from asthma and gave a lovely example of patient endurance, and to me was often an inspiration. Sister Colman developed a heart condition last year. Sister Bridgettine had a very bad and prolonged case of pleurisy. She rested, and now is on three hour duty with civilian internee patients here. Sister Robert Marie did a lot of catechetical work with lay people. Sister Redempta and most of St. Paul's Hospital staff worked at Santo Tomas hospital with internees, at St. Pablo's and then at Los Baños. Others manned the annex of Remedios Hospital. Sister Frederica's list of works bears her own inimitable stamp. Normal College Sisters organized classes for Sisters and did private teaching. St. Mary's Hall finally ended with a staff of two—Sisters Claver and Concepcion. Sisters David Marie, Marie Aimee, and Philomena

Marie, who are with us now, were there during Assumption days. Sisters Maura Shaun and Clotilde, as in 1941, are doing shifts in the hospital. Almost all are terribly thin and have little vitality after the starvation era. But now with good food and the memory of God's mercy, we all feel wonderful! I would say that is no exaggeration. I am trying to confine myself to Sisters—though I'd love to tell how wonderful our Army is!

O Mother, what tales you'll hear of your interned daughters. We gathered cocoanut shells; hoarded coffee grounds, tin cans, used-tea leaves! We often amuse ourselves with skits (à la Sister Maria del Rey's inspiration) concerning our life of captivity. We've learned to go stockingless, discalced, to wear wooden shoes (bakias): line up for roll calls till we are sick of them; to wade through mud, lug water, go without it, to do without breakfast and dinner; to endure tropical sun, dirty clothes, and water shortage. The last straw came when we were given raw *palay* (unhulled rice) to eat as there was no way to get firewood for our stoves of every unpatented type. Now, we are in the B.B. (beri-beri) stage of things; but it is wonderful to be free, though we are in a first class jail.

I tell you this, with not one sigh of regret in having had to bear it. Thank God and you, Mother, for sending me here. It was the least I could offer whole-heartedly—though I'd take a full meal anytime!

Thus Sister Maura Bernadette limned in the picture of life in enemy territory. It was written in the white heat of exaltation following the dramatic and daring rescue of over two thousand internees from Los Baños.

The years were long for those interned in the Philippines and for those anxiously awaiting word of their well-being. Fifty-three Maryknoll Sisters were stationed on Luzon when the Japanese attacked. Nine of the number were in Baguio, Mountain Province, and from their convent eyrie, they witnessed the initial landing of the Japanese at Lingayen.

It might be asked why in the face of warnings, the Sisters were not recalled to the United States. Since the beginning of the Sino-Japanese war in 1937, missioners in the Orient found their work becoming increasingly difficult. Maryknoll Sisters had been under fire in the Shanghai 'incident.' Concerned about the many, though isolated, situations which were curtailing the Sisters' mission activities in the Far East, Mother Mary Joseph in 1940 made a mission visitation. It was October 10th when, on the *President Coolidge,* she sailed out of picturesque Honolulu harbor, bound for Yokohama. Conditions there were very tense. In a letter to the community dated January 1, 1941, she writes:

We arrived in Japan at a time of crisis—to learn of much that had passed without our knowing it—chiefly and most seriously affecting the declaration of a totalitarian system of government with all the evil it brings. How far reaching it is to be no one yet knows. . . . The day was spent in discussing affairs—and came to a close so soon—with so little accomplished and so much left unsaid.

Mother Mary Joseph was courteously but firmly advised by the various countries she purposed to visit that she would not be permitted to go beyond the port cities. By cable, she summoned superiors of different mission sectors, and representatives of the various works to meet her at the ports most convenient for them. Every one was able to keep the rendezvous, not without some difficulty getting out and greater ones returning. The letter mentioned above continues:

We left Yokohama and our missioners there Saturday evening. The next morning found us at Kobe, around ten o'clock—in a torrential down-pour. Restrictions on allowing visitors on board boats while in harbor are very strict—yet both the *President* officials and the Japanese took pity on the Maryknoll Sisters who had come to meet us from Manchukuo and Korea in the North, and from nearby Kyoto. They were allowed to remain with us all day. We were able to talk over freely conditions and we mapped out general courses of action to be followed in emergencies.

That the emergencies would arise soon, there was no doubt. Mother Mary Joseph recognized that the times ahead would not only try men's souls but test their trust in God. She foresaw difficulties for her daughters—not the least of which would be to preserve the calmness required to make considered judgments in the midst of confusion and to maintain the clearness of vision to see and to evaluate emergencies properly. Father Walsh, Maryknoll's loved Father Founder, had enunciated this fundamental doctrine of his sublime Faith on the eve of his first departure for the Orient in 1917—"The sooner we who aspire to the life of missioners realize the wonderful Providence of God, the better it will be for us all." With like confidence Mother expressed the policy to be pursued in face of danger: "It is the spirit of our community, and my desire that the Sisters remain at their posts unless actual catastrophe were to drive them out." This basic principle is so strong that the Sisters freed from internment immediately set themselves to the work nearest to hand. In the Philippines this readiness to get back to the job so impressed a Staff Officer in the Seventh Amphibious Force that he wrote to friends in the States, under date of April 21, 1945:

> These nuns have been through HELL—yet there is absolutely no recrimination—just joy and happiness at their well being and that they have an opportunity to pick up their work and start again from scratch with not a personal item in their possession and not a cent to their name. I now have a new concept of the Foreign Missionary.

Something of what it costs the Leader of the Maryknoll Sisters to accept the sacrifice of her daughters-in-Christ finds rare expression in a letter addressed to the families of the Sisters whose health made it possible for them to remain for the reconstruction:

> "Blood is thicker than water" we know and believe, but the spiritual bond that unites me to my "children" is strong and enduring and I long, too, quite as much as you do, to see with my own eyes just how they are, to talk with them and be with them. I say this only to assure you that I appreciate your disappointment and longing.

It was some time before the information was given out that the Los Baños internees had been moved behind the American lines to Muntinlupa. Here was a jail, finished just before the fateful December 1941. It made a safe and far more comfortable retreat than foreigners of the allied nations had enjoyed in many months.

On February 24, 1945, the day following the release, these letters were written to Mother Mary Joseph. They reached Maryknoll on March 12th.

From Sister Trinita, Regional Superior:

Loving greetings from the forty-seven Sisters who were at Los Baños. You probably know more about our rescue than we do, as we hear it was broadcast to the States.

The Army is taking very good care of us, and after a few good meals, we are already looking and feeling better. God bless our boys—they are wonderful—can't do enough for us. We are the first of their kind they have met since Guadalcanal and they are anxious to talk about their folks at home.

A brief calendar will give you an idea of our movements during the great silence.

Jan. 13, 1942—All Sisters except Baguio group interned at Assumption College.
Sept. 15, 1942—Eight Sisters went to St. Paul's Hospital to help out. The Spanish Dominicans in charge.
May 15, 1943—Six Sisters, interned at Baguio, transferred to Assumption. Sisters Hyacinth and Carmencita are not able to stand the lowlands because of health, so Sister Andrew was allowed to remain as nurse, and also Sister Una, who is a neutral.
Sept. 15, 1943—Sisters Constance, Scholastica, Marie Bernard returned to Baguio.
April 11, 1944—Sister Trinita a prisoner to Fort Santiago, Manila.
April 26, 1944—Sister Brigida a prisoner to Fort Santiago, Manila.
July 9, 1944—All Religious, American, British, Dutch interned in Los Baños.
Aug. 18, 1944—Sister Brigida transferred to Philippine General Hospital from prison because of health.
Jan. 1, 1945—Sister Trinita transferred to Los Baños.
Feb. 23, 1945—Rescue from Los Baños.

From Sister Mary Brigida,

Thanks be to God we have come through safely. Just now the camp radio announced that the internees at Los Baños have been liberated! All the Sisters have been there since July with the following exceptions: Sisters Una, Hyacinth and Carmencita, who are in Baguio. Of these we have had no news since January. Sister Concepcion and Sister Claver are in Santa Ana, Manila, with the Spanish Charity Sisters. Sister Trinita and I have been separated from the Sisters since April when we were taken as prisoners to Fort Santiago. A letter from Sister Constance (then in Baguio) was caught by the Military Police who could not interpret it. The letter written in diary form gave news of Baguio—our Sisters and friends. The military wished us to identify everyone mentioned. They compile lists and then go after natives who are friends of foreigners. We therefore did not comply lest our benefactors be endangered. In August I was transferred to the Philippine General Hospital as I was very ill. I was there during the bombardment!

I am now with the American Internees at Santo Tomas (University) camp, enjoying real bread! and butter! and milk! and regular meals. God bless Uncle Sam!

Sister Trinita? She stayed on at Fort Santiago for nine months when there was some transfer. We heard that she went to Los Baños but there is extreme doubt of the matter. We must hope that she has not been killed, hope until we have proof. When I get in touch with the Los Baños folks, I'll send you news of her at once.

Whatever the most extravagant of New York newspapermen have to tell of Manila events will be mild in comparison with the reality.

The remarkable restraint in these letters can be appreciated fully only in the light of the information contained in a letter written by Sister Brigida on the following day and in subsequent messages from Sister Trinita and the other Sisters.

Sister Trinita is safe with the other Sisters from Los Baños. Perhaps she has gotten a message off to you also, but I'm not taking chances. Hundreds of people have been inquiring for Sister Trinita and will rejoice in her safety. Imagine my relief after hearing for weeks of her death; some informers went so far as to say they saw her body—others, a Maryknoll Sister's body, etc. The place has gone mad with rumors of all kinds.

From Sister Trinita—March 9, 1945:

There are now fifty of us accounted for. Sister Brigida came to us on March 5th, from Santo Tomas. She is well. Sisters Concepcion and Claver arrived here March 6th. They left St. Mary's in flames, on February 10th, and had a hard week going from place to place, dodging fires, bullets and sentries. They finally reached the Spanish Sisters of Charity. The Colonel in charge here admitted them temporarily as refugees, but I doubt if there will be any follow-up on them, as I explained there was no other place to which they could go.

All our places in Manila—St. Paul's Hospital, the Normal College, St. Mary's Hall are destroyed. St. James Academy, Malabon, is intact but Sisters from Manila sought safety there with their charges. No one has penetrated as far as Lucena.

Sister Concepcion and Sister Claver, native daughters of the Philippines, were not included in the ban on foreigners. Until the last moment, when at the imminent approach of General MacArthur's men, the Japanese fired the city, the two Sisters remained at St. Mary's Hall, guardians of the property stored there. Sister Concepcion gives an account of her stewardship, and discloses simply the spiritual outlook that makes it not only possible but necessary to pray for one's enemies.

Sister Claver and I are still alive. When we left St. Mary's to escape the raging fires all over the neighborhood we thought we would not see any one of our Sisters again. We haven't yet. But will. We are dying to be with them after being deprived of community life for eight months. Not but these dear Charity Sisters give us of their charity beautifully. Maryknoll lost everything, Mother, and the Filipinos have suffered untold miseries. Once when Sister and I were flat on the street for one hour with shells overhead and bullets all around, we thought that was our end. We accepted death and offered our lives for the conversion of the Japanese. That is our vocation!

Greater love hath no man than he lay down his life for the spiritual good of his enemy.

The letters from the Sisters do not attempt an historical narrative of the progress of the war, but they give pictures of their lives as enemy aliens, and they continue on to recount the efforts of those who are working now toward a reconstructed Philippines.

Sister Rose Genevieve, in a letter written three years and three months after the attack on Manila, telescopes the events of the first days:

It was early morning December 8, 1941, when word came of the attack on Pearl Harbor. During the night of the 8th and 9th, the first bombing of the Manila sector began. At St. Paul's Hospital, we received casualties from Cavite and the Piers. December 13th, our organization and personnel moved to Philippine Women's University on Taft Avenue, about two miles south. There a 400-bed hospital was set up. Army doctors were in charge, and we and our nurses worked with them.

The city was in a turmoil. Huge fires burning at Pandacan and Cavite as well as the bombing and destruction of Sto. Domingo Church, Sta. Rosa and Sta. Catalina in Intramuras brought terror to the hearts of many.

On Christmas morning, the personnel of the hospital assembled to hear the announcement that the American Army was withdrawing from Manila. The sincere offer of the doubtful haven of Corregidor or Bataan did not extend to the native nurses, so the Sisters elected to remain with the girls. The officers reluctantly accepted the decision. They promised to return in *three months,* and told the Sisters to hold the hospital. With this parting of the ways imminent, no one had too keen an appetite for the traditional Christmas dinner menu of turkey and sauce!

Sister Justin relates the story of that departure:

At four in the afternoon all the American wounded were ordered out. By six most of them were on the way to hospital ships and Australia. At seven, Captain Barry, his sergeant, two army nurses, and about twenty men were ready to leave. The Sisters stood in the great hall to bid them Godspeed. The Captain repeated his offer—"Sisters, if you want to come with us, we will take you."

Sister Redempta's face was haggard from fatigue and the weight of responsibility. Sister Bridgettine's anxiety for her nursing school students was apparent. We all realized how empty the huge place would be with only our two priests, ourselves, the nurses, and some two-score Filipino patients. But our duty was to remain. The Army must be on its way. As the last one departed, the priests bolted the doors. Thus they elected themselves our porters.

The Sisters in Lucena were in the direct line of march to Manila from Legaspi where the Japanese landed. The weeks that followed December 8th were full of foreboding for them. The movement on the main road grew. Trucks and tanks filled with soldiers headed one direction, caramata, carratella, carabao carts of the natives went the other way. Sister Aquinata states laconically:

We heard of the attack on Pearl Harbor and of those close at hand—Baguio and Legaspi simultaneously. Schools closed immediately and we waited for developments. As the enemy drew near our town, we were evacuated on Christmas Eve, under a barrage of machine guns and bombs. Enemy planes studded the sky. On the morning of December 26, 1941, Lucena was in Japanese hands. Escape No. 1. At midnight 24th–25th, we were unmercifully bombed in Manila at St. Mary's Hall where some of us had taken refuge. Escape No. 2. Next we moved to our Normal College. Then Manila was declared an open city; the American Army moved out; and all Maryknollers moved into the Army hospital, the former Philippine Women's University, to await the entrance of the Japanese into the Queen City. What days of doubt and fear as to the possible fate of the white population!

It did not require the knock and the cry, "Open in the name of the Imperial Army," to tell the Sisters that the Japanese soldiery were without. On the afternoon of January 2nd, the invading force entered Manila and part of it settled down opposite the hospital emergency building. It was two the next morning when the authorities got around to interning the occupants and posting guards. Sister Aquinata continues:

I saw the first Japanese entering the city. The trucks came up Taft Avenue from the south; flags flying, soldiers grim and quiet, and very orderly. We heard from them the following morning at 2 A.M. They interned us and left guards.

During the following days the Japanese military made repeated calls about taking over the building. The Sisters' offer to care for the wounded was dismissed. True to life, amusing incidents helped lighten the burden of the times. Sister Rose Matthew narrates this with humor:

A soldier asked for a drinking cup. He looked at the trade mark "Made in U.S.A." and rejected our offering. The next cup he examined only to read the legend "Made in China." He marched off—patriotic and thirsty.

On the evening of January 11th, the military police stomped in with blades flashing. The Sisters had received permission from the proper authorities to evacuate the native nurses to a place of safety. The guards did not understand, and thought a mass escape was in progress.

Sister Aquinata continues her account:

Sister Bridgettine and Sister Isabel, together with two doctors, and the Filipino house boys, were lined up in the patio. The rest of us were kept in the foyer which opened on the garden. We were all ordered not to stir. A machine gun was set up on the threshold and trained on the group in the court. When a soldier squatted behind it, I decided it was all over for us. This scene was held for two hours—eternities it seemed. Then an officer from the Bureau of Religious Affairs walked in, snapped commands, and the police were happy to slide out quietly. Sister Georgia had managed to notify the Jesuit house that we were in trouble, before the phone was knocked out of her grasp. The Jesuits contacted the Committee. Throughout the war, we often questioned among ourselves the why of this Bureau of Religious Affairs. It seemed to have extraordinary power, and was helpful in cases where the military became too adamant. You will note, Mother, that I had ceased counting escapes! I was singing the mercies of the Lord.

This little scene marked the end of the stay of the Maryknollers there. Next day, under guard, the Sisters were interned at nearby Assumption College. It was a goodly mob—forty-three Maryknollers with about twenty-four of their St. Mary's girls, and two Sisters of the Holy Cross. Sisters Olivette and Caecilius, en route from Indiana to India, were stranded in Manila by the war. They were frustrated in their efforts to reach their destination, but their mission initiation was without parallel! It was to this group that Reverend Mother Rose and her Assumption Community opened their doors and their hearts, and with whom they shared their possessions. The freezing of funds had made cash a very cold proposition, indeed, for Americans. But the charity of Filipinos and neutrals was spontaneous, delicate, warm, and enduring!

To the comparative serenity of Assumption College, the bombings of Corregidor and Bataan, were undertones that told of little peace on earth. And when these sounds ceased, the quiet was even more disturbing! Wisdom dictated that it was better not to imagine all the human anguish bespoken by that new and awful silence.

The Sisters turned to the safe refuge of work, of study, and of prayer. The set-up of the College was ideal from the point of view of the internees. One entire wing was placed at their disposal. This provided dormitory space, not more crowded than Maryknoll Sisters are accustomed to—each cubicle was the width of a bed and a chair; it provided also a community room, refectory, and a kitchen. The pews in the centre of the chapel, between the choir stalls, were reserved for the internees. Like *The Man Who Came to Dinner,* these guests remained unconscionably long. It was not their fault, but their good fortune, to be at Assumption from January 12, 1942 to July 8, 1944. For the first six months the Sisters were formally confined. In July 1942 they were ordered to report to Santo Tomas Internment Camp where they received instruction and permanent releases. This meant that they might engage in approved non-income producing activities outside the College during the day, but must report there at night. Later the second proviso was relaxed in favor of Sisters nursing in hospitals.

The unconquerable will of the Sisters that this internment be not the waste lands is one of the arresting features of their saga. First there are the intangibles—the deepening and the mellowing and the ever-growing virility of the spirit, and the strengthening of the community bond. Then there is the intensely practical approach to the problem of establishing a normal way of life under abnormal circumstances.

Again and again the Sisters' letters give testimony of a charity that bears all things for the conversion of the oppressors, for the spiritual good of the stricken peoples, for the work of Maryknoll and the well-being of their beloved Mother General. One would rather be guilty of counting the streaks on a tulip than of trying to imprison in print the delicacy of these sentiments. Not one Sister has failed to express in one form or another the thought of Peter on the Mount of Transfiguration—"it is good for us to be here." The vocation which sent each one into danger was tried and found to be sound.

The first day at Assumption College, an horarium was evolved which provided hours for prayer, work and relaxation. This schedule was subject to adjustments, as the nature of the internment changed.

Book by book, the entire library of the Maryknoll College was transported to Assumption by the faithful Filipino house boys. Laboratory facilities were at hand. The College staff was complete. Sister Caritas, Dean, inaugurated serious class programs. The Sisters applied themselves to studies they needed for credit or took refresher courses.

Two of the Sisters had completed at Santo Tomas the Ph.D. class requirements for their degrees. They had finished also their research work for their dissertations. The internment, they devoted to writing them. For Sister Colman's *Comparative Study of Classic and Romantic Tragedy* with particular attention to Sophocles' *Oedipus Coloneus* and Shakespeare's *King Lear,* tragic, brooding Manila was not unsuited, but as a backdrop for the *Critical Estimate of Dante Gabriel Rossetti, Poet and Painter* by Sister Miriam Thomas it was a study in contrasts.

Sister Clotilde's apostolate was in training native catechists. The work began with a group of young people sent to Assumption from the Malate parish. It was soon noised about that Sister was giving a course in Religion Methods and pastors from all over the city enrolled their catechists.

On the entertainment side—Sister Maria del Rey wrote skits and directed her company of amateur actresses. She gave piano recitals, classic in selection and professionally rendered. If music were the flow of soul, the dramatic efforts were the feasts that helped keep reason controlled and balanced.

It was not the best time to take up the culinary art. From the earliest days food was a problem. At Santo Tomas, the internees received supplies, but this was not the case at Assumption. A strict rationing was observed from the first. The Assumption Sisters were most kind; the Jesuits exercised a paternal care; the Filipino friends were generous out of all proportion to their material resources. Every act of mercy the Sisters had performed in their two decades of devoted work was repaid in this time of tribulation. Sister Frederica who ran for years St. Jude's Patronage, a medical service for the destitute, glories in the gratitude of her dear poor:

"Sister, you had my teeth pulled for me and new ones put in. That's how I could get work because I was ugly before. Here is some rice."

"Sister, you bought me glasses, I couldn't see, but then afterwards I could iron. I am making money. See, we pay you back now!"

"My first baby was blind and died, Sister. But my second one has good eyes because you gave me milk and medicine and put me in the hospital. We could not forget and we had our marriage made right. God has been good to us. Let us help you now."

Every Sister had the same experience. Our people loved us; they tried to care for us. They were faithful beyond anything we ever dreamed them capable of, and courageous as well.

Sister Trinita sounds the same note in her letter of April 16, 1945:

Perhaps the Sisters in their letters have told you how wonderfully kind our Filipino friends were to us through the long years. I think the Sisters will agree when I say the most generous and helpful of all were Miss Caterina Jamias and the two faithful house-boys at St. Mary's Hall. One of these boys was shot that awful night when our two Filipino Sisters, Miss Jamias and the boys had to leave the burning building.

They remained at the Hall even during the Japanese occupancy. Miss Jamias and the boys went from market to market each day trying to get sufficient food for us, and then helped to prepare it.

Shortly before I went to Fort Santiago, Miss Jamias went to her home province, supervised the harvest of her rice crop, had it husked by hand, and arranged for its transportation to Manila by bancas. All this involved a risk few had the courage to run. Then she gave it all to us, fifteen sacks. At that time, rice in the black market was 300 pesos a sack.

There was the house-boy in Baguio—well trained, and a treasure, worth a wage that would put an American into the income tax class. Community funds were at a new low. Gregorio's abilities were not unknown to the wealthy families in Baguio. They made tempting offers for his services. The Sisters advised him to accept for his own economic welfare. But he declared he would remain with the Sisters so long as they needed him. He maintained this attitude and later attended the Sisters into the American lines.

This loyalty was so marked that the Philippines emerged from the war a nation bearing it as a special character. She paid dearly for this seal. It cost her the destruction of her Queen City, Manila, the demolition of her summer capitol, Baguio, the ruin of her villages and countryside "from Aparri to Jolo." It cost her in the first seven months of the war twenty-eight thousand of her youth. For it she put her women in mourning and let her children go hungry. She paid with her architectural treasures—her churches centuries old. The people's unshakeable faith in General MacArthur's last promise—that he would return was a part of this loyalty. The native spirit of *mañana,* which in good times often tried the patience of Americans, was reassuring. He would come—on some tomorrow!

Already plans for a new Manila are under way. The old traveler will return some day. He will recall with a certain nostalgia the little streets with their countless Chinese bazaars; he will tell of the picturesque houses with galleries that stretched out precariously over narrow walks; he may reminisce about the nipa hut villages outside the city—colorful, but comfortless; he will, it is devoutly to be hoped, be able to rejoice over an industrial district worthy of man and aware of the dignity of labor. He will stride along broad boulevards, discourse upon the Malaysian touch in the new architecture. May he look deeper, into the soul of a people. Not upon—modern plumbing—is a civilization built, but upon the principles of a common brotherhood, established in God, the Universal Father.

In the summer of 1944 most stringent internment laws were promulgated. Sister Colman reports:

On July 7th, while the Sisters were at supper, two members of the military police came. They assembled the Sisters and read the order from Tokyo that all were to be interned the next morning. When Sister de Chantal said that Sister Bridgettine and Sister Colman, who were ill, could not be moved, they would not give a definite answer. It was a busy night. Everyone was allowed two suitcases, or bags, and also her bedding. The Assumption Sisters offered to help in any possible way. Sister Concepcion got push carts and transferred perishable things to St. Mary's. Sister Assumpta and Sister Marion Cecilia had gone over to St. Paul's for a couple of days, and we pitied them for bags packed at the kindly discretion of others are of questionable value in normal times, and these times are not normal. The Assumption Sisters were kindness itself. They worked with us until long into the night. We had a lunch before midnight. A few canned goods that had escaped the can opener bent their necks at last to the steel blade.

Word got around that we were going to camp, and our friends gathered early on the morning of the 8th to carry away anything we might wish to give them for safekeeping. Some books, linens, records were gotten out before our armed captors arrived in four trucks. They brought a doctor with them who wrote out a permit for Sisters Bridgettine and Colman to remain at Assumption "until recovered". The Assumption Sisters took them into their own infirmary and lavished every attention and care upon them. The Japanese were ahead of schedule, and were anxious to get off. They treated us courteously, and helped with the baggage. We took the army beds and mattresses which we had brought to Assumption with us. We feared that the soldiers would be angry when they saw the crowd that had gathered, but they seemed little concerned. The people slipped money into our hands and tried to give us little packages of food, but the soldiers said, "No food." The superior of the Belgian Sisters came to lend any possible assistance. She took a *carretela* load of the most valuable of the College books to St. Teresa's. Before noon the trucks drove off. As they passed the gate, the soldiers lowered the curtains so that the people in the streets could not see who the new captives were.

The last truck went to St. Paul's to get the Sisters there who had received their summons about the same time that we heard ours. The Dominican Fathers were most solicitous. They gave the Sisters a money offering and enough porcelain plates for the whole group. They had the truck cleaned and hospital benches were put in. Father Lopez gave each one his blessing as the Sisters left the building.

When the trucks reached Santo Tomas, we lined up for baggage inspection. We had no contraband goods and hence little difficulty. They were searching for any kind of written material especially. Dinner was served at noon, some rice and a kind of vegetable stew. In the afternoon we were ushered into the gymnasium, 500 of us—missionaries all—priests, Brothers, Sisters, scholastics, and Protestant ministers with their families. Sections of the floor were marked off for the different groups and suwali mats spread out to sleep on. (When Sister Bridgettine and Sister Colman were en route to Los Baños, they spent from Saturday to Tuesday under like circumstances.) About 4:30 a meal similar to the noon one was served. At seven o'clock we lined up for roll call. Another count was taken at nine. Then we made an effort to settle down for the night. Some of us brushed the mosquitoes away while others made a pretense of sleeping for an hour or two. The brushing and sleeping relays continued during the night, but the brushers were always in the majority; for the mosquitoes, the heat, the hard floor, and the poor restless babies, had "murdered sleep."

No one needed a second invitation to arise when the guards called us at 2:00 A.M. Sunday morning. It was our first Sunday without Mass. At 2:40 breakfast was served—lugao (soft rice) a kind of hard-tack bread, and a hard boiled duck egg. Roll call was taken again, and before three o'clock we were formed into ranks, first in two's then four's, and finally into single file and marched to the thirty waiting trucks. We were crowded into the closed trucks and taken to the train through the dark streets. As daylight came, we saw that the station was crowded with Filipinos who had evidently spent the night there, hoping to squeeze themselves into the packed coaches in the morning, or even to ride on top of the cars.

When they spied the trucks they tried to see us, but our guards did their work efficiently, and no communication was established between the outer world and ourselves. We were finally put on the train, and about ten o'clock we reached Los Baños station—our last internment camp—at times we thought it would be our last earthly encampment.

It cost us much leaving that blessed haven, the Assumption Convent, where we could live our religious life so quietly, still we felt a sense of relief in being taken to camp. For the sword of Damocles had hung so long that its very shadow had grown sharp. It had struck twice already when first Sister Trinita and then Sister Brigida were arrested and taken to the awful Santiago prison. Now that it had fallen on the rest of us, the suspense was ended.

3

The Fruit of the Spirit

THE glorious feast of Easter 1944 was celebrated with pomp and ceremony in the beautiful chapel of the Assumption. The Alleluia dominates the liturgy of the paschal season. The minor chords of remembered sorrow are muted, but they are there to ears attuned. Easter Tuesday's Mass reminds the faithful: "The Lord is risen from the *sepulchre, who hung for us upon the tree,*" and again

> It behooved Christ to suffer, and to rise again from the dead the third day; and that penance and remission of sins should be preached in His name among *all nations.*

Here is the missioner's *raison d'etre.* It is the explanation of Maryknollers' presence throughout the mission lands, and the motivating principle which makes them hold to the task.

Easter Tuesday, 1944, fell upon April 11th. About eleven in the morning, at Assumption College, where the majority of the Maryknoll Sisters were interned, the police were announced. The attention of the military always aroused great fear. The forgotten man is the fortunate one in war zones. Sister Trinita was the object of their inquisitional interest, an interest that was not satisfied by minute cross examination, nor by meticulous scrutiny of her borrowed home and her scant possessions. About noon, Sister was led away. Her destination was not disclosed, but the presumption that it was the dreaded Fort Santiago proved to be correct. Exactly two weeks later, almost to the minute, the scene was reenacted and Sister Brigida was removed.

Fort Santiago was a dungeon, built into the old wall centuries ago when Manila needed to be fenced in, for reasons of protection, from the Moro raiders and the Chinese pirates. It remained something of an antique, its harsh features softened somewhat by the tropical blooms which graced the old court. Young banana shoots with their fresh green leaves, flaming poinsettias, on stalks all of eight and ten feet high, seemed stenciled on the gray walls against which they carelessly leaned. The delicate yellow plume of the acacia tree watched its still reflection in the fountain bowl. Violetta hedges stood as sentinels along the paths. Great rose colored bouquets were the adelfa bushes flanking the broad stone staircase which led from the patio to the dread examination chamber above. And hidden at the very roots of one was a tiny patch of small star-like flowers—the sampaguita. One knew it was very brave to be there, for what the thistle is to Scotland, the shamrock is to Ireland, the sampaguita is to the Philippines. The whole scene was heartbreakingly lovely, and almost shattering in its appeal. Sister Brigida always felt that here was the proving ground of her steadfastness. Life was more precious away from the dark, crowded, ill-smelling dungeon. And in the very early morning hours, as she was led across the garden to mount the steps to the judgment hall, Sister Brigida recalled its beauty, and sometimes the sweet fragrance of the *dama de noché,* or the stronger odor of the ilang-ilang tree wafted from some nearby street came to her, doubts crowded upon her, and she recognized this as her garden of Gethsemane.

Under the caption, "The Story of Fort Santiago," the newssheet, *Free Philippines,* in its issue of March 3, 1945, runs an article from which the following excerpts are taken:

The following is based on interviews with several prisoners at Fort Santiago.

The military police took the prisoner to the fort. Inside the main gate, he was taken into the headquarters of the military police, where he was carefully searched. Everything he had, handkerchiefs, papers, pocketbook, money, keys, etc., was taken away for examination and deposited. If the man was dismissed, they were returned to him.

There were four cells near the desk where the man taken in was searched. Into one of them the prisoner was thrown. If there were several, each went into a separate cell so they could not compare notes and match stories.

Later the prisoner was taken into another part of the fort where there was a row of cells, not too narrow, not too wide, and into one of them he went and did not come out again except when he was removed for questioning and what went with it; picked and privileged to take the pail out; sentenced, or released. Those in the cell were packed close. At night when a man lay down to sleep he could not move till morning. During the day each sat on his haunches the Japanese way. He must not talk.

The food was not fattening. A handful of rice, squash if there was any, "kankong." That was all and it must do. Aside from the systematic starvation a man underwent, when he came out he usually bore, again aside from the marks of the beating and burning, a skin disease from the condition of the cell.

Those who were taken in for questioning were beaten, burned with cigarette butts, slashed, or filled with water to almost bursting and then struck a heavy blow in the pit of the stomach. . . .

Each was taken out of his cell again and again and questioned relentlessly for hours. Every angle was covered by the investigation. If one did not answer well it might be the last thing he'd ever do. It was good tactics to admit some guilt.— . . . If one insisted on complete innocence the investigation and beating might go on indefinitely.

This pen picture nowise exaggerates what the Sisters endured in Fort Santiago. The charges brought against them were espionage, helping the guerilla, connecting with American submarines, and encouraging the Filipinos in their attitude of resistance toward the invaders. There was no proof for such accusations. Interrogations that usually began in the hours just after midnight were based on the stated assumption that the Sisters were guilty otherwise they would not be in prison. Yet a confession of guilt was demanded relentlessly.

Father Russell Hughes, the first Maryknoller to return to the States after the retaking of Manila, tells the story of the Sisters:

We learned that Sister Brigida and Sister Trinita were taken because the Military Police had captured what they considered an American spy. This person was a woman, a refugee of the Nazis whom the Japanese suspected of carrying messages for the American guerilla forces. The day she was taken, she carried letters from Baguio to Manila for many people. All these people had been picked up and examined. One of the letters was a small greeting from the Sisters in Baguio to the Sisters in Manila. It was addressed to Sister Trinita and mentioned the receipt of a letter from Sister Brigida. We also learned that Sister Constance, and rumor said all the Baguio Sisters, had been taken to Baguio's jail. This was later confirmed.

While the reason for the Sisters' arrest was thus explained, it seemed a blind. The Japanese would often use a very flimsy excuse to take some one and then try to crack him upon their suspicion of something else. With typical indirect approach, the Sisters were accused of acts they could deny. Undoubtedly the Japanese were aware that there were leaks in and out of the Prisoner of War Camps. They might have heard vague rumors that connected Sister Trinita with the efforts to assist American soldiers. It is certain, they wished to trap the Sisters into naming persons which might afford them clues. Heroically and at the cost of measureless suffering, the Sisters never allowed a name to escape them.

Maryknoll Sisters in the Philippine Islands have been under the direction of Sister Trinita for many years. Sister is a capable administrator, a prudent leader, a wise counsellor. She possesses a temper that flares at injustice and strikes out at its perpetrators. The warmth of her personality makes friends wherever the force of her condemnation of unfairness has not made enemies. Her Japanese guard to Los Baños returned to Manila to get a bag and supplies for Sister from St. Mary's. Another, whom she had known when he attended Father Cummings to the Assumption in Manila, was so distressed at her appearance when she arrived at camp from Fort Santiago that, from his own small pay and at great personal risk, he brought her gifts of food. "She was so kind to me in Manila" he would murmur.

After a score of years in the East, Sister remains as American as the sidewalks of her native *heath.* The Logue sisters, now

Sister Trinita and Sister Luke, were born and reared in old New York. If ever the records of the police in Manchuria come to light, one will find Sister Luke's address, given solemnly, day after day as Pennsylvania Station, New York. "I didn't bother explaining that one of the telephone booths probably marks the sight of our old home" she remarks. Today, Sister Trinita's convent has some features of a depot. A chaplain writing September 1945 says:

The effects of long days in the prison camp are gradually leaving and their ugly memories are fast fading. This is due in a large extent to the fact that the convent has almost turned into a Grand Central Station. The fellows are anxious to spend their free time with the Sisters and as you know they forget about everyone else and tell the Sisters all about their folks and the girls back home. Sister Trinita is an authority on the love life of young soldiers and they love her.

To one of sympathetic nature, the events in the Philippines were crushing. But Sister Trinita rose above this weakness to give to the oppressed the fruit of her spirit—a Christlike service. Father Hughes knows better the story of Sister's help to the imprisoned Americans than anyone:

I do not know the whole story as I was merely an onlooker. Besides that, in the days of the Japanese occupation of Manila, for purely personal-security reasons, one had few confidantes, even among one's most intimate friends. Not from fear of betrayal, but often the zeal of one's friends was embarrassing and revealing.

Sister Trinita was not one to make a great display of her works. During the years after she had first been made Regional Superior, the Maryknoll community in Manila had slowly and gradually progressed to recognition among the top flight. Her lack of flair was ideal for the work of the underground and Sister was in a way one of the leaders of one branch of the underground. The surrender of Bataan was a crushing blow, but it was only a prelude to the terrible "Death March" from Bataan to Cabanatuan. The plight of these Americans, due to unnecessarily harsh treatment by the Japanese, aroused the feelings of Americans and Filipinos. Neutrals and nations of Nazi-invaded countries were also aroused. The feeling was "let us do something—but what?" The Japanese let it be known they would allow no contacts between prisoners and outsiders.

The prohibition of the Japanese was only an incentive to these people and was besides heartbreaking to the motherly Sisters. Immediately plans were laid and medicines and food gathered from hidden caches. It is not known, but I later discovered, that Sister Trinita became the focal point for the gathering of supplies. More than that, she interviewed salesmen and suppliers and arranged to introduce them to interested parties who would pay for their goods. A system of transportation was organized among the many girls that Sister could contact. Medicines and altar supplies began to trickle into the camp at Cabanatuan. This, of its nature, could not remain a small thing. It had to develop and grow. Neither could it be limited to the immediate need of the poor soldiers that survived the Death March. The prisoners had to be cared for during the three years of captivity and the underground worked till the end. I can not say Sister Trinita was the leader and sole organizer of this branch of the underground, because by its ramifications and the need for secrecy it had many and silent members. But I do know that her name accidentally turned up whenever I contacted members. It usually slipped out in the casual reference, "All right, Father, I'll see if Sister Trinita has it." Knowing Sister Trinita was a Maryknoller and Padre Hughes was also, they presumed too much. The underground railroad was a funny thing and had many peculiar angles to it. One had to walk charily. But it worked successfully and its members suffered tremendously either by physical torture inflicted by the Japanese, or mental tortures self-inflicted by fear.

Sister Trinita was always working for the Prisoners of War. I often tried to hint that she "lay off" for the risks were great. My reward was a smile and a murmured "poor boys." On one occasion she accompanied a non-Catholic lady to the office of the General in charge of American prisons. The attempt was made to secure official permission to send needed clothes and medicines to the various camps of American soldiers and prisoners. They were harshly rebuked and ordered to leave. In the foyer of the building a scowling, sulky Japanese officer approached and gruffly asked if she wanted to help the Americans. Sister assured him that was her purpose. He told her to walk slowly up Daitoa Avenue (Taft Avenue), past St. Rita's Hall. Wondering and fearful she and her companion, a gray-haired woman of sixty, did so. Presently a truck came along. It was an old U. S. Army truck taken on Bataan and had a big passenger cabin over the engine. Some one hailed the Sister from the cabin; it was the Japanese officer. He invited the two in, and drove off. On the way up Daitoa, the officer asked Sister her address and wanted to know if she could feed four American soldiers. It presented a problem, but Sister was equal to it. A quick look at her companion, a nod of the head and an agreement was reached. They gave the companion's address. The truck stopped at the door and, after Sister and her friend had alighted, drove off.

To agree to feed four or five men during the hungry war years was a fine, charitable impulse natural to one of Sister Trinita's motherly instincts and a patriotic gesture to her friend. But to gather food, and it would have to be other than rice, was not easy. Sister went back to the Assumption, and put it up to the community. Miracles happened then. Some Sisters went out to the stores, some went to friends' homes, and some went to the Sisters' cupboard. Noon came, and the festive board was heavily laden with a delicious home cooked American meal. Possibly most of it had once lain in cans, but then who would be disdainful of canned food when one had eaten only rice for months. Shortly after twelve o'clock the truck appeared and the Captain of the Imperial Japanese Army herded four ragged, dirty American prisoners of war into the house. There followed some moments of embarrassment when the soldiers saw white women, and those women Catholic religious. This, however, did not last long under the skillful management of the hostesses. The "boys" went off to wash, and put on their new dry clothes. Then the meal, smokes and talk. The Japanese, though, had to watch the time and cut short the conversation. He had requested medicines and clothes for the camp. The other Sisters had been busy collecting these and on the soldiers' assurance to Sister Trinita that the officer was a "right guy" she turned all over to him. With promises to bring others in turn on another occasion, he gathered the men and drove away.

Such was life in Manila during 1942 and 1943. Sister Trinita and the other Sisters did what they could for the American soldiers. It was dangerous and left everyone under the continual fear lest the Japanese discover their activities. The virtue of charity drove them on and sustained them. These were the corporal works of mercy in action to a degree seldom given a community of Sisters to perform—and paid for at a great price.

Four months of imprisonment, almost nightly interrogations, repeated torture, broke Sister Brigida's health but not her spirit. She was transferred, still silent, from Fort Santiago to the Philippine General Hospital, on August 18, 1944. She was to return to prison upon recovery, but the kindly Filipino doctors and devoted nurses never reported her sufficiently well. A Hawaiian newspaper carried an anecdote which may refer to Sister Brigida. The police could elicit no information from a Sister under examination. The conversation went like this:

You are an American?
Yes.
What was your father?
Irish.
What was your mother?
Irish.
There you are, Irish, as stubborn as the Archbishop of Manila!

No one ever went voluntarily to Fort Santiago. Sister Redempta and Sister Rose Marie (gallant sister of Father O'Callahan, S. J., hero chaplain of the Carrier *Franklin*) are the exceptions that proved the unbroken if unwritten law. They courageously—even though in fear and trembling—called at the prison in an unsuccessful effort to send Sister Trinita and Sister Brigida a change of clothing. The officer received them courteously, perhaps he was amazed at their temerity, but he regretted he could not comply with their request—it was not the custom of the institution!

Sister Trinita was released without warning or explanation on December 31, 1944. Asked if she were hungry, by a high ranking Japanese official to whose office she had been taken, she warily replied, "I am making no complaint." Food was given her, and she was permitted to rest. Very late that night, under guard, the only woman in a troop train, she left Manila for Los Baños. For eight and one-half months, Sister had no contact with the outside world, nor any consolations of religion. Once she was in the court at the water trough, when she recognized two priests who were being brought in. Sister had been deprived of her habit so there was no mark of identification. As she threw water over her face she whispered her name and asked for absolution. One of the priests seemingly raised his hand to his hat, made the sign of the cross and murmured the *Absolvo Te.* By some miracle of grace, during the long months of trial she retained her serenity of spirit, helped greatly to sustain the morale of her cell mates, and managed to keep a perfect account of the passage of days, and months.

The two victims of war offered themselves as oblations that the Japanese might be "converted and live."

> Who then devised the torment? Love.
> Love is the unfamiliar Name
> Behind the hands that wove
> The intolerable shirt of flame
> Which human power cannot remove.
> We only live, only suspire
> Consumed by either fire or fire.*

* T. S. Eliot: "Little Gidding"—*Four Quartets,* Harcourt Brace.

4

The Yankee in the Camp of Los Baños

"MAYBE it would look all right if I stand on my head," said Alice in her Wonderland. In the process of rescue from Los Baños Camp, the internees were transported by amtracks across fertile terrain, onto the waters of Laguna de Bay, thence behind the American lines to Muntinlupa. Tanks taking to the water like ducks were a novel development to persons who had lived in most restricted areas completely cut off from outside contacts. If not religious dignity, then physical weakness restrained the Sisters from experimenting with the idea that, viewed from a reverse position, the phenomenon of tractor ferries might be resolved.

This experience they were to find was but an initiation into a changed world. A Commander wrote back to the States in 1945: "It took some time for them to realize that WAVE differeth unto wave, the curl, and wave, the ocean heave! Sister Marcella speaks of 'small automobiles that we Rip Van Winkles find to be *jeeps*.'"

Their passage from Los Baños into this new world was dramatic and fraught with peril. On the morning of February 23, 1945, the inexorable, execrable seven o'clock roll-call was approaching when the sound of roaring motors distracted the internees. All faces were uplifted to the skies. Despite the custody-of-the-eyes ruling, promulgated by the guards, every one watched every plane. The only ships flying were American. The very shadow of the wings of a good old U.S.A. bomber gave a sense of protection. This morning the planes flew not in battle formation, but wing to wing. They swept in low, over the camp, circled, gained altitude—and suddenly the heavens burgeoned forth parachutes! In a cracked second, firing started. That not a single gun was Japanese, the internees learned later.

Under the cover of night, American Infantry and Filipino guerrillas had penetrated the enemy lines some twenty-five miles and surrounded the camp. The appearance of the paratroopers was the prearranged signal for the land forces to launch a concerted attack on the guard houses. The complement of each of the eight posts was eight men. Wholly unprepared, the sixty-four guards on detail went down simultaneously. American soldiers and the guerrillas poured into the compound. Roll call was postponed automatically, indefinitely. Several of the priests left the assembly line and went toward the chapel. It promised to be a busy day and they first wanted to offer the Holy Sacrifice of the Mass. Some of the Sisters followed. Sister Marie Bernard narrates:

> The flames of the tracer bullets licked past the windows. We prostrated on the ground—the chapel did not boast a floor—and took up the recitation of the rosary. Then we heard distinctly from the other side of the suwali fence, a few feet away, but out of our vision, a voice unmistakably from the deep South drawl an order. The accent carried to us a wealth of reassurance. Soon he appeared, this superman, dressed in fatigue suit and surrounded by short stocky native guerrillas carrying rifles as long as themselves (it seemed).
>
> "Are you all right, Madres?" queried one of the guerrillas solicitously. But before we could respond, he continued, "Down with the Japs," and ran on to avenge upon the invader his country's wrongs.
>
> We were told the plan to evacuate as quickly as possible and burn the camp behind us. Even as we packed the bag we were allowed to carry, the battle continued and I have marveled since at how calm everyone was in the midst of flying bullets. Only two of those entering our barracks of ninety-six persons made any impression. One shot to pieces the cup Sister Frederica was carrying to Sally Silan, a young girl who had been shot in the hip. Sister Rose Genevieve gave first aid to the girl while Sister

Frederica shook splinters of china from up her sleeve. Sally went out with the stretcher cases to recover behind the American lines.

The protection of the Blessed Sacrament is always the first thought in times of danger. Sister Rose Matthew relates:

I arrived at the chapel—among flying bullets—just in time to help consume the Blessed Sacrament. There were no ceremonies thereafter, I assure you. I just ran for the amphibian tractor where I rested in peaceful joy on some baggage and made my thanksgiving.

Word concerning the dire plight of the internees at Los Baños had been carried to the American forces by some who had made good their escape from the camp. There seems to be foundation for the belief that the day that saw the rescue was to have witnessed the death of the prisoners. The retribution was complete, realistic. Sister Maura Bernadette writes:

The entire Japanese garrison, two hundred and forty-three men, was wiped out. We left the camp dragging our luggage down the road as, on either side, the barracks crackled and flamed. We were put in tanks which tore through abandoned villages where fruits and foods were weighing the trees and earth down. We who had been systematically starved—told: "Everyone is starving—even your own soldiers."

There was a fleet of amtracks. According to the boys the first one was designated "Sisters Special." That this rescue was made in the heart of enemy country is pointed by the strafing from hidden positions on the shore, of the tanks as they traversed Laguna de Bay. But the internees turned refugees felt well protected with American wings forming a canopy above, and American soldiers beside them.

So many of the boys wore rosaries about their necks, a Sacred Heart badge pinned to the uniform, a medal of our Blessed Lady on a chain. If all were Catholic, then the Catholics outnumbered greatly any other religious group. Superstition? Colonel Romulo ascribes to Maryknoll's heroic Father Cummings the oft quoted sentence: "There are no atheists in fox holes." Sister Beata's tribute is but one of many paid by the Sisters to the American soldier:

> We are all admiration for "our boys." They are magnificent, and one is not surprised that they are looked upon at least as minor gods by so many of the people! They are certainly grim looking fighters, but they relax very easily into the usual cheerful good-humored American. The day they performed the daring and difficult task of our rescue, they were as nonchalant and unperturbed as could be imagined—so much so, that most of us hardly sensed the great hazard of the undertaking, and went off as if on a picnic.

The action paraphernalia of soldiers includes a supply of concentrated foods. This is the C-ration Kit. Although the boys were working under strain and against time, they broke their kits and supplied the internees with their own rations. One feels that this simple action was a modern military parallel of the ancient rite of breaking bread, with all the symbolic significance of friendship implied. In a post-war story, an English professor of the classics is made to find the nectar and ambrosia of the gods in American pancakes and maple syrup. To those released from Los Baños, dehydrated foods rated equally as high in flavor.

When it became mathematically impossible to allot foot space to another prisoner at Santo Tomas, the Japanese had established this internment center at Los Baños some forty miles outside the city. The site was part of the Philippine Government's Agricultural College. Located in a fertile valley, on one side of it rises Mount McKieling, with summit wrapped perpetually in a mantle gray; on the other is Mount Banahao, its luxuriant bamboo forests shining green in the sunlight, bending gracefully in the storms.

Emotion recollected in tranquillity may be the stuff of poetry. Sister Colman does not think much of it as a basis for good reporting. She prefaces her story of internment in Los Baños with these remarks:

> The story of our sojourn in captivity must begin with a twofold apology; first, it is an inverted narrative, written largely in

retrospect, and as such it will not tingle and throb with the hopes and fears that would have animated a contemporary chronicle; and second, it will have necessary lapses and inadequacies in the record since all notes had to be destroyed at different danger points and crises. The scribe has attempted to patch together the scattered memories of the principal events with the kindly aid of all whose powers of retention have not been too badly shattered by bombs bursting in air and by a diet warranted to produce cadaver appearance.

In preparation for the arrival of the missioners, a split bamboo fence was erected to segregate the newcomers from the eleven hundred internees already in residence. It was not long before old-timers dubbed the new section "Holy City" and the other, in contrast, "Hell's Acre." Internee labor had been used to erect the one-story buildings with their wooden frames, suwali sides, and nipa roofs. This 1944 housing project called for ninety-six to a barracks. The furnishings consisted of the army bed and the assorted suitcases each person was allowed to bring, and the contraband things each one managed to smuggle in.

Maryknoll's Father Russell Hughes and two Jesuit Scholastics performed the jobs that defied the carpentry skill of the Sisters. Thanks to the ability of the former to discover wood and nails, their dexterous handling of saw and hammer, their prodigal use of time and strength, shelves were installed in the Sisters' cubicles; stools and chairs were constructed for their comfort. When a porch was added to the barracks, Maryknoll-in-Los Baños was the finest dwelling in the enclosure!

The colony, girdled by eight guard-houses, consisted of twenty-eight buildings as alike as New York's brownstone fronts. In addition there were the Japanese headquarters, a hospital and kitchens—these latter just that much waste space after the starvation regime was inaugurated. An infirmary annex became necessary and one half of a residence barracks was turned over for this. One building was headquarters for the American Internee Administration Office, a second was used for meeting hall and classrooms, another for the Protestant chapel and library, the fourth for the Construction Department, and a fifth for the Catholic Chapel of St. Joseph. The space between the last two named buildings became the cemetery. The corporal work of mercy of burying the dead was done by the Jesuit Scholastics as a labor of love, but digging the graves took great toll of their daily depleting strength. Sister Patricia Marie writes:

During the last ten days or so at Los Baños, we had a death a day, and the strain on the Jesuit Scholastics was so great that we feared they themselves would drop into the shallow graves they dug.

Here to God's Acre were committed the mortal remains of many loved ones—perhaps no one was more generally mourned than Father Mulry, S.J.

Los Baños with its two internee Bishops, its more than three hundred Priests, Brothers and Sisters, and its lay congregation of between six and seven hundred, had the unique distinction of being raised to a diocese. His Excellency, the Apostolic Delegate for the Philippines, Monsignor Piani, issued in September, 1944, the official letters erecting the *Prelatia Nullius* of Los Baños Internment Camp, and named the Right Reverend Bishop Jurgens as Bishop and Monsignor Casey as Vicar General. Probably no other diocese so small territorially ever existed, nor existed for so short a period! It was about this time that the camps were amalgamated.

The first concern of the religious was to prepare a place where Christ in the Blessed Sacrament might make His abode. The cubicles were removed from that half of the barracks which had been turned over for chapel purposes. Sister Colman writes:

A main altar was built from local lumber and installed. We worked busily all the day. A plaid curtain which the College Sisters had brought was hung as a dorsal behind the altar; a plaid shawl donated by someone else formed a canopy. The tans and browns of the plaids blended with the suwali walls and gave a pleasing, rustic effect. The Lucena Sisters brought forth a carved wooden crucifix to hang over the tabernacle. The tabernacle itself was a Mass kit. One of the Dutch Sisters remarked,

"This is, indeed, the camp life when even God is to live in a suitcase." The Franciscan Sisters made a decorative veil for the improvised tabernacle. Some vases were made from bamboo tubes to hold the wild flowers that grew nearby, and a small statue of Our Lady of Maryknoll was placed in a niche in the wall at the right of the altar from which she smiled down on us until we received a native one of Our Lady of Antipolo.

In the other half of the chapel, twenty-eight small altars were erected. Here over a hundred priests offered Mass daily.

A shortage of altar wine and wheat flour was always a very real anxiety. On one occasion the Japanese Committee on Religious Affairs sent the wheat. A minimum of altar wine was used by each priest. It was measured and dropped into the chalice from a medicine dropper. Instead of a large host, the priest consecrated a small one for Mass, while those distributed in Holy Communion were broken into tiny particles.

Benediction of the Blessed Sacrament was given every afternoon. High Mass was sung on Sundays and feast days. As time went on, one realized the effort it was for the priests to carry out this program because of increasing weakness.

Sister Caritas takes up the theme:

One of our greatest consolations was the Divine Office, especially during those months when we were privileged to sing Compline in our chapel at Los Baños. The Dutch Sisters recited the Little Hours publicly; the Franciscans said Matins and Lauds in choir. Ours was the great joy of chanting Compline, the official night prayer of the Church, for the Religious internees!

To set up even light housekeeping was a struggle. The barracks of the Maryknoll Sisters, being on the end of a row, fortunately provided them a degree of privacy. Between every two barracks were lavatories, but the water pressure was so poor that even a slight trickle was hailed with delight. At night, if a gurgle was heard, the Sisters rose in haste to perform their ablutions and do their laundry. The Jesuit Fathers eked out the meager supply by hauling water a great distance, so every effort was made to conserve as much as possible. Los Baños should have been interpreted as Lost Baths.

Sister Marie Bernard's description of the "settling-down" process is more of a standing-up program:

We soon fell into line and practically lived in one or another of the various camp lines for the duration. If you chanced upon a line the purpose of which you were ignorant, you claimed a place; afterwards you inquired as to the why and wherefore. Bit by bit, we acquired our oufits—straw hats, wooden shoes, wash tubs, tin pails, enamel plate, knife, fork, and spoon, native stoves, earthen water jugs, trays, stools—these were all necessary parts of our equipment. Our collection of tin cans and cocoanut shells came gradually and as the need arose. By the time we were freed, most of us had a sizable collection both in quantity and quality.

In the beginning, the most welcome thing was a stool. You felt a certain degree of liberty of motion, when you did not have to depend upon an immovable bed for a chair.

The first week in Los Baños the food for the Religious was prepared in the lower camp and sent over. The menu was—

Breakfast: Corn-rice mush and thin cocoanut milk. Twice a week there was a pale amber drink euphemistically named coffee.

Dinner: Rice or lugao, and a vegetable stew.

Supper: The same, usually. Infrequent variations might be camotes (native fibrous sweet potatoes) instead of rice; a boiled vegetable—as green papaya, or squash, or camote leaves, or konkone (a tubular stem like a waterlily's). Once in a while a piece of carabao meat was detected. It was established that a single pig provided the essence for stew for two thousand internees.

Later, a kitchen was allotted to the upper camp. But even the Jesuit cooks could not make good meals without materials. They served, however, humbly, with great good humor, and exquisite sensitiveness. "It was real torture to ladle and scrape when serving two scoops of watery rice to half starved nuns," wrote a Scholastic, to his sister at Maryknoll. "The spirit in which the nuns went through it all was an inspiration. Cheerful and laughing—never down and yet suffering visibly from all the effects of beri-beri. . . . You can be very proud of them, very proud indeed." The truck gardens, communal and private, encouraged at first by the Japanese, provided some of the needed green vegetables. But this activity was frowned upon later. To the end, a few internees cherished cocoanut shells in which sprouted anemic-looking salad leaves.

On September 21, 1944, carrier planes of Admiral Halsey's Third Fleet struck at Manila, and the internees knew the Americans were fighting their way back. By that time food rations were very light indeed. The first of October, dinner was discontinued. Thereafter meat became a memory. Rice in very limited quantity was the not-too-stable food. Sister Scholastica says:

It would have made excellent glue were it not so wormy! Some of these worms were almost an inch long. I guess we should not have minded them since some people actually went out and picked slugs and cooked them up. Those who ate them said they were good.

All of us picked pigweed and lutoe, two edible weeds, for our craving for greens was intense. We were very prudent in trying out wild growths. It called for restraint but we had practiced this virtue from the first. Our unwritten law was never to eat all of the food we received, no matter how little that "all" might be. We always saved something for the next day.

At the end, palay—unhulled rice—was dispensed. It is not Japanese custom to feed those who are about to die.

Next to the ever-pressing question of food, clothing was the greatest problem. The Sisters had bivouacked in many spots, and in each move something was lost or had to be sacrified. Material for replacement of habits could not be bought. While interned at Assumption College, Sister Trinita had made nurses aprons out of sheets, like those worn by the hospital Sisters on duty. This was a blessed foresight. Habits were reserved for chapel wear only. Aprons were full dress for all other occasions. Time came when stockings were likewise conserved. Shoes were out and were replaced by the native bakias. These are on the order of mules, but the soles are of wood and the tops of straw braid. One clops along, and when roads are muddy one, perforce, steps out of the clogs and proceeds barefooted.

Sister Miriam Thomas writes to Mother on Easter day, 1945:

During our days at Los Baños my task was to help mend the clothing of the clergy. Several Sisters from each community patched and darned and finally attempted a few tailoring jobs. A pair of trousers which began its career as custom built, ankle length, proceeded on to Huckleberry Finn type and finally resolved into shorts. From the scraps of material gained in the shortening process, Sister Alphonsa raveled thread for sewing. Finally old curtains, laundry bags, shawls, were converted into shorts or shirts.

Much of the activity of the camp grew out of the necessity of supplying the most elemental economic wants—food, shelter, and clothing. All internees over fourteen years of age were required to do a minimum stint of two hours a day. The men collected wood, stoked kitchen fires, cooked, did construction and outdoor clean-up jobs. The women gardened, prepared vegetables for camp meals, in small groups recooked the meager fare to make it less unpalatable, or added to it the products of their little patches; they made brooms and worked on sanitary commissions; they sewed and laundered the fragile garments with immense care. Until the Japanese cut the electric wires, the Sisters did a pressing business with the iron they always included in their traveling impedimenta. Nursing the sick was a shared labor. Sister Agnes Regina's account reads in part:

A water shortage and crowded living conditions caused an epidemic of bacillary dysentery so we were called into service to help care for the "emergency" and we remained on—caring for other cases. "Our" two Holy Cross Sisters, two Immaculate Conception Sisters, four Maryknoll Sisters, an English Quaker nurse, a Seventh Day Adventist and a Methodist nurse together with two Jesuit Fathers, a Dominican Father, an Episcopalian Bishop and a Seventh Day Adventist school teacher as orderlies constituted the "staff" of the Annex. One of the interned Navy nurses was liaison officer for supplies as we were not permitted to talk to members of the other camp. It was a good working group under the sacrificing, fighting Doctor Nance. The Episcopalian Bishop made an excellent orderly—he had been administrator of their big hospital in Japan until it behooved him to move elsewhere.

There were works of supererogation. Some Sisters did social visiting among the flock of Maryknoll's zealous Father McCarthy. Others helped in the library, in the canteen while it ran its fluctuating career, still others taught in the grade school. In turn most of the Sisters became students again.

Father Monahan, S.J. gave a series of enlightening conferences on *The Canticle of Canticles.* Father Mulry named the course he gave to the Sisters *A Cyclorama of English Literature.* His reputation as a teacher *par excellence* was well established in the Jesuit Order and appreciated in the Island. He also gave some talks on Post-War Education in the Philippines. Even as he planned, one wondered if he would lead in the new paths. Four months in Fort Santiago had not helped a physique that was already spent. Sister Justin writes of Father's last sermon delivered on the Feast of Christ the King:

> Father Mulry's crown of glory is his last public conference given from the altar steps of the tiny cathedral chapel of St. Joseph, Los Baños. His text was the inspiring Preface for the feast. His diction was superb; his cry for "a kingdom eternal and universal, a kingdom of truth and life, a kingdom of holiness and grace, a kingdom of justice, love and peace" was no longing for a surcease of pain, but an expression of indomitable faith that the world of individuals, the world of nations, can be restored only in Christ. It was Father's last great gift to us and one of unsurpassing holiness.

After the camps were merged, a mission was preached. The Sisters visited the barracks to interest Catholics in the services. It was successful from the point of view of attendance, and for the number of lapsed Catholics who returned to the Sacraments.

Los Baños was not on the circuit of American troupers! The great Hope—was for American troops! The priests and Brothers formed a glee club and Sisters gave inter-community entertainments on the feast day of each order. The unity in diversity of the Church was exemplified in the oneness of spirit which animated the Religious of different communities. Name days were observed. Gifts were ingenious, personal, and wrought with care

—a tin can with handle of braided weeds, a small rattan board to stand on in the improvised shower, a tray bearing all the marks of being hand done, a beautifully polished cocoanut shell. At Christmas—a small green tree trimmed with *silver* ornaments, cut from precious tins, delighted old and young. The crib, its figures modeled by a Dutch Brother from mud and baked to a genuine copper hue by the tropical sun, was as great a surprise and gave as deep joy as could St. Francis' original creation. A guard brought flowers for the altar. Hand-painted greeting cards, the work of Sister artists, were exchanged. Maryknoll's Sister Miriam Thomas copied the altar of the Chapel. The significant inscription was from the office of First Vespers of Christmas—"Lift up your heads: Behold your redemption is at hand." But rescue was far enough off to allow for the return of Sister Trinita from Fort Santiago, for the celebration of the silver jubilee of the canonical erection of the Maryknoll Congregation, and for the campaign of intensive prayer which was the prelude to release.

Early January 1, 1945, Sister Trinita arrived in camp from Fort Santiago. The priests, Brothers, and Sisters in the camp had made constant intercession for the safety of the Religious imprisoned in Fort Santiago, Bilibid and Muntinlupa. Describing that New Year's morning some two months later, Sister Mary Catherine writes in a breathless style:

> Oh! what a grand and holy New Year's Day—for all of us, when we could collect ourselves and stop brushing away the tears of joy—and some of sorrow! Sister was so sad a sight—her eyes sunken, face pinched (she had lost over eighty pounds), skin diseased, suffering was written on every feature. She was so composed that she made us all feel ashamed. Sister was very glad to see each one of us—and was able to reach up and put her arms around each one, and kiss her, and ask how she was, and say some little personal thing to each one—with no thought of self. We sang a great *Te Deum.*

The temporary withdrawal of all but a handful of guards was the next four-star event. Rumor was they had gone to meet MacArthur! In fact, that week, he did lead the first landing on

Luzon! January 6–11, 1945, will be known to all internees as *Liberty Week* but for reasons non-military! Los Baños was located in a land of plenty. So soon as the Japanese disappeared, the Filipinos appeared laden with fruits and vegetables. The improved diet gave all a lift. Because of the perishable nature of the goods, a tropical climate, and no refrigeration, it was impossible to put in a supply. When the Japanese returned on the 11th, hunger and ruthlessness ruled the camp. Life was not lived for long on the hill tops, but in the monotony of starvation by degrees.

Sister Antoinette is responsible for this story of Liberty Week:

Our Filipinos came to us as soon as the guards disappeared, bearing gifts of food. It was hard to believe our eyes, but the thing that flapped was a chicken, and she was ours! Her name? Henna, of course! We were too great realists to allow visions of Southern fried to dance in our heads. A modern Philip said "But what is one among so many?" With the wisdom of a Solomon, one decreed that it should be kept, fed worms from the cereal, and lay—not golden—but hen eggs for Sister Trinita! And so it fell out!

February 14, 1945, marked the silver jubilee of the canonical erection of the Maryknoll Sisters Congregation.—"Our hearts were all at Maryknoll" writes Sister Ancilla Marie, "we wouldn't let starvation dampen our day." According to Sister Trinita:

Bishop Jurgens would have the day fittingly observed. And all the Religious cooperated heroically! At great physical cost, our Maryknoll Fathers sang a Solemn High Mass and also gave Solemn Benediction of the Blessed Sacrament. They were so unfailingly concerned for us. The dozen different communities of Sisters presented an exquisitely painted spiritual bouquet of one thousand Masses heard, Communions, Benedictions and Rosaries. The priests and Brothers representing fourteen orders or congregations, made a rich offering of Masses said or heard, and of Holy Communions received. There was something very touching in their efforts to make a folder. On the cover was a picture of Our Lady with the sweet inscription "Dearest Mother, protect your congregation."

For feast day fare, we had hoarded some flour for muffins,

canned apple sauce, and tea. We made the day as festive as possible, and we were all very happy, and ignorant of the events taking place in Manila—

The events to which Sister Trinita refers were the killing of so many Religious and native Filipinos; the stubborn resistance of the enemy—the house-by-house, street-by-street fighting; and the mopping-up operations. The increased hostility of the guards gave clew as to how the battle was going.

Under starvation, sickness, death, the spirit of the camp was low. Euphoric compensations are not found in beri-beri. In this extremity, Bishop Jurgens ordered a novena in preparation for the feast of Our Lady of Lourdes, February 11th. The Americans took Manila, but the internees at Los Baños were still "in the protective custody" of the Japanese! The Bishop ordered another appeal to Our Lady of the Rosary. There were to be three days of exposition of the Blessed Sacrament, and the rosary was to be recited continuously. The Maryknoll Sisters were privileged to initiate the triduum—February 22nd. It was evening of the first day. And on the morrow a hundred and thirty-five American lads dropped from the skies. "They looked like angels, their delicate rayon parachutes as wings ruffled in the early morning breeze!"

It was of Los Baños that General Douglas MacArthur wrote in his communique:

Nothing could be more satisfying to a soldier's heart than this rescue. I am deeply grateful. God certainly was with us today.

5

Patterns in the Grass

In the order of time and of military importance, the taking of Manila by the American forces precedes and supersedes the Los Baños episode. Military communiques, amplified by radio commentators and news correspondents, gave the picture of events as seen from the American side. Three Maryknoll Sisters were in Japanese-held Manila, but outside intramuros. Sister Brigida was a patient in the Philippine General Hospital, in the Ermita district; and Sisters Concepcion and Claver, both Filipinos, were at St. Mary's Residence Hall, in Paco, when the Americans began their return engagement. At the end, the three Sisters were under the insecure roof of the hospital. From February 3rd to the 17th, Sister Concepcion made day-by-day notes. The diary does not treat of military movements. It is merely a human interest picture of civilians caught up in the tide of war:

February 3, 1945. We slept little last night because of the guns and crackling of fire from the Paco section. It sounded like a battle was being fought outside Manila.

February 4th. This morning, Esteban, our boy, brought news that the Americans arrived and took Santo Tomas and Malacañan Palace and Pandacan. We are afraid to hope it is true. Fires.

February 6th. News scarce. Much shelling and blasting. Fires spreading. We believe that the Japanese are trying to get rid of their ammunition. Nobody dares cross the street lest the sentries shoot. One shell hit on our house. A hole in the roof.

February 7th. We begin to clean our wooden buildings, in hopes our Sisters in concentration may be home soon. Shelling, and blasting, and close at hand, the strange sound of the machine guns.

February 8th. House across from us struck. One man killed, one injured. Sister Claver gives first aid. Much noise, thick smoke and the smell of burning things.

February 9th. Fires coming our way. We prepare bags for departure if necessary. Another hit on the wooden building. The fire brigade, composed of our two boys, ourselves, and the rain, put out the blaze. A second hit—this time the concrete building—all glass shattered. A big fire from San Marcelino heads toward us. The Bureau of Science is aflame. A fire from Taft Avenue looks as if it is moving this way. Will the three meet at St. Mary's?

February 10th. We tried to get a little sleep, sitting in chairs, taking turns watching the progress of the fires. After midnight, the Cosmopolitan Dormitory caught fire, the flames sweeping down to the apartment houses between Taft and Pennsylvania Avenues. We decided it was time for us to go. Our own Miss Jamias and our boys went with us. We spent some time in the Christian Science shelter. The wind changed the course of the fire—we moved again. Mrs. Wang on her way to her brother's house with her three children invited us along. Machine gun fire. We fall to the earth. Esteban shot in ankle. We all made the house where we stayed until early morning. Sister Claver and I decided to try to reach the Assumption Sisters in Madrigal's house. Met Dr. Garcia—told us Madrigal house was burned three days ago, invited us to his home, and warned us not to cross streets. Plenty machine gunning. We breakfast at Garcias about ten A.M. We try to get a little rest—but a shell injures a young girl in adjoining room.

February 11th. Late last night when fire started across the street, Doctor told us to climb rear wall and be ready for escape if necessary. Hundreds gathered in the gardens and watched the blaze. People trampled vegetable patches they used to watch so carefully! About four A.M. everything looked safe and we returned, to sleep in spite of shelling. It never stops. We hear that the Japanese are starting fires everywhere. Sunday—but no Mass. The Spanish Consulate afire and flames licking this way. We move again. Movements always in packs as everyone is trying to get away from something. Machine gunned. We prostrate on street, shells over head, rocks falling from the ruins, a shower of bullets around us which lasted an hour. A shot—and the Chinese man lying at my feet is killed. To my right, Judge T. shot. When it is over, the Japanese marines march us single file to the dispensary, but some girls are taken by them. Miss Jamias' niece is gone. The dispensary is an *eight minute walk* from St. Mary's, but it took us *three days* to make it! The men separated from the women and some of them we hear are killed. It is so sad—no family without missing members.

February 12th. We slept in sitting position on floor—so crowded we could not stretch out our legs. Lugao for breakfast. Sister Claver offers to help in minor injuries. So little to work with, she gives her First Aid Kit. A narrow escape, when a window near which she is standing crashes in.

February 13th. News that our St. Mary's is burned! Shelling, shelling—but we know that is American. The great fires are not! Dead and missing people! We try to comfort the suffering and sorrowing.

February 14th. This evening, because of fires, all ordered to Philippine General Hospital. Sister and I hold tight to each other and to our bundles as we stumble through the streets. In the mob, we are afraid we may get separated. The road covered with broken glass, rocks, looks funny in the flames. At the hospital, we are sent to information, then to floor three, and we are an overflow, but someone knows us and crowds us in. Sister Brigida is in the building somewhere.

February 15th. We see plenty of American planes in the sky and hear rumors of American tanks! Some incendiary bombs start fires in the hospital but are put out.

February 16th. We sleep around like waifs. Last night in one of the corridors, the night before in a shower section. Sleep is not the right word—people only nod. We made the opportunity to go to confession this afternoon. Sounds of street fighting.

February 17th. Holy Communion this morning. Most awful shelling. We are told not to leave the ward—then comes word for us to go to the nurses' home. The people panic stricken. A doctor asks, "Please, Sisters, go ahead and lead the people." We pass the information place and out of the corner of my eye I see big men in olive colored soldier suits—the Americans are here! We walk out of the hospital. The Americans direct us to walk on ahead. Taft Avenue looks like Pompeii must have looked. At a distance, we see the ruins of dear St. Mary's. We must have got into Oregon Street. It is difficult to tell where we are. In a group of officers, we recognize a chaplain. We introduce ourselves and tell him of Sister Brigida. He promises she'll be cared for. When we look up we see a motion picture machine turned on us. It scares us almost as much as the guns we'd faced. We are so tired and have no place to go, so many convents and churches are burned down. Our poor Manila! We feel sorry for ourselves, but a Jesuit Brother comes along and brings us to *La Ignaciano.* We are given something to eat and then the pastor takes us to the Sisters of Charity. There Sister Brigida comes for overnight, and we talk and talk.

The next day Sister Brigida was taken to Santo Tomas. She relates concisely the last days at the Philippine General Hospital with dangers threatening from every side:

We formed the front line of battle from the 7th to the 17th of February. The enemy retreated towards the building from all sides, slaughtering, and kindling fires en route. They had three *huge* guns around us, the one on the nurses' home being less than two hundred feet from the ward that I was in. There were nights of terrible suspense when we expected to be machine gunned in the wards. Several times I made the short act of "Acceptance of Death," wondering if I could finish it before the end came—as the walls rocked around us, plate glass shattered, shrapnel wounded this one and that; and our bodies grew numb from the concussions. An old Spanish, two-story house (which was left standing when the hospital was built around it), blazed. It was about twenty feet from the hall of the ward in which I was confined. The roof of the upstairs ward caught fire. After some time burning debris came tumbling down the stairway at the door of the ward. We decided to chance the machine gun bullets whizzing past our door. We all cleared the place just before the roof crashed. It looked as if we were to die but we might select the ward which would witness the scene!

During the terrible barrage of guns at the entrance of the hospital, we lay flat on the floor, we refugees, Chinese, Filipinos, Germans, Jews, Spanish, Americans. I, unfortunately, had no alternative but to lie down in a dirty puddle on the floor. When the barrage was over and I arose, a little nurse offered to clean up my tunic as it was all mud. I went to the bathroom and changed into a hospital apron.

As I stepped out into the hall in my clean garb, a man near me shouted, "The Americans are here!" Was I so muddy as to have been unrecognizable before as a compatriot? The crowd began to murmur, to shout, to cry, to push, in their joy, and panic was threatened. A Jesuit scholastic elbowed his way to me and asked for support on a rosary which he began shouting above the din. I did my best to shout too and soon the hysteria subsided. All prayed; even a Jew near me murmured—"Holy Mary, Mother." An order came to go to the Nurses' Home outside of the hospital. We feared to obey. Were the Americans really there? Then somebody spied two lanky soldiers with bayonetless guns placing themselves to guard our path. They were grinning cheerfully and chewing gum! There *was* no mistake! We filed out, the stronger of us helping the weak and wounded. Many of the rescued kissing the boys' hands, and their clothing, and a few of our own women like Mrs. B, gave them a big hug and kiss. One of the lads removed his helmet, in a gesture of deference to me! I almost followed the ladies' example when I saw that his head was as red as my own. Wouldn't he have been surprised!

* * * *

It is a Romany custom for caravans to leave a sign of their passage.

> Where my caravan has rested
> Flowers I leave thee in the grass.

The mission vocation calls its followers to the cross roads and over the trails of the world, regardless of distance, heedless of dangers. Their footprints do not always form a pattern that the world can interpret.

When war threatened in the Far East, Baguio, the city in the hills, because of its protected location, gave promise of being the one place in all the Philippines that might expect to sit out the war in peace. But it was destined to live up to its name: In the Tagalog dialect Baguio means storm. On December 8th, within a few hours after Pearl Harbor Japanese bombs rained upon it! Thereafter, the planes that flew over the city daily were not friendly. On December 24th, Baguio was Japanese territory.

The Igorots, in whose barrios the Sisters had worked, crept into the grounds, and begged the Sisters to go into the mountains for safety. However, with the exception of twenty-four hours in a concentration camp, the Sisters remained in their convent until November 1943, when six were interned permanently. Two sick Sisters were left under the care of a third Sister. Sister Hyacinth of New York, Sister Carmencita of Manila, and Sister Una of Ireland by way of Boston, managed a bare existence in Baguio until December 26, 1944. When the city became the storm center for the returning Americans the Sisters took to the road and found shelter with the Igorots in Tuba, seven miles distant. For almost two months they lived in nipa huts and later in the natural caves.

The huts are two-room flimsy buildings made from the palm leaf, interwoven with the sturdier bamboo for support. Either one or both of these rooms are raised on stilts which necessitates entrance by a three-rung ladder. The floors are of split bamboo. The houses within present a clear, if not clean, appearance as furniture is rarely to be found, and clothes are below the minimum requirement. The *sala* is a living room in very truth. Here the family regardless of size, in a space probably six by six, sleeps and lives. Over a brazier, in the smaller room, the cooking of rice and fish is done. Of the Sisters' life in Tuba, Sister Carmencita writes:

> Below us on the hill we found the Adoration Sisters. Two Dominican Fathers, whose house in Baguio was bombed, came later and occupied a neighboring hut. Our little convent was in the best condition, so it was chosen for the daily offering of the Holy Sacrifice.
>
> For some time we felt quite secure. It was on March 6, 1945, that we got our first scare. Breakfast was barely over when a dozen bombers appeared suddenly, hovering rather low.
>
> Our faithful Igorot boy, Gregorio, had dug a hole for the storage of food, as there were rumors about looters in the neighborhood. After we saw the bombers, we immediately crawled into that hole! No sooner were we inside than explosions, machine gunning, and all kinds of terrific noises made us sure that our last hour had come.
>
> Some time later, between the bombings, one of the Adoration Sisters came over and begged us to go to the rescue of their Sisters. We ran to their hut and found four Sisters already dead and two dying. Four Japanese soldiers were coming down the hill behind the convent-hut and were spotted by the American

bombers; a projectile missed its target, exploded close to the hut, set fire to the kitchen, and killed the Sisters.

The Fathers buried the victims in the hole made by the bomb. Our fragile hut was too unsafe for further occupancy; so we moved our few belongings into one of the natural cave shelters. I wish we had a picture of our home in the rocks—a real Bethlehem one! Holy Week came and we were advised to move on. But where?

A heavy downpour of rain on Easter Sunday proved our cave not water tight. At four in the afternoon, we walked some distance downhill, reaching an evacuation center at seven in the evening. We hadn't gone to that place in the beginning, because it was in a malarial section and was very crowded; our cave had been cleaner and more secluded.

For two days and two nights and well into the next day, the refugees, numbering about five hundred men, women and children, slid down rocky defiles, struggled and slipped across a swollen stream, clambered up volcanic cliffs, holding on to scraggy pine twigs, grasping clumps of coarse grass, leaning on walking sticks. Stops were made only for food and snatches of rest. The hazard was twofold, risk of accident because of the rough terrain, and the danger of meeting Japanese patrols. The Maryknoll party made it a practice to travel in formation: first Bessie Acab, the Igorot woman, then Sisters Hyacinth and Carmencita, followed and watched over by Sister Una. Gregorio brought up the rear. Sister Hyacinth was showing unsuspected powers of endurance. Her strong will seemed to inform her frail body. On the afternoon of the third day, when the caravan reformed after a brief stop at Ambusi, the little party became separated. The road was quite clear. There was no reason for alarm. About an hour later, when she came to a stream, Sister Una stopped and waited for her companions. The water was tumbling wildly enough to have been purified. Sister Carmencita arrived and was glad to cool her face. Together they awaited Sister Hyacinth and watched the weary people pass. When only stragglers were left, the Sisters grew alarmed, and Gregorio went to meet the wayfarer. His trek brought him back to the resting place of the afternoon. Sister Carmencita continues:

The caravan had gone on. But we waited—over three hours—for Gregorio's return. He reported that he had found no trace of Sister Hyacinth. Darkness was coming on, so we continued our journey. At last we reached the river where the whole caravan was delayed on our account. The guide to whom we reported Sister's case assured us that there was a shorter trail by which she might reach the next mountain, for which we were headed.

It was too late for the caravan to proceed that night. So we slept on the rocks, and started out at about seven the next morning. We arrived at Pitugan—into which the shorter trail from the Ambusi hut led—on Thursday night. There was no sign of Sister Hyacinth.

Friday morning at ten we limped into Tubao, safe inside the American lines, but with what heavy hearts! Without losing a minute, we reported Sister Hyacinth's disappearance. The officers immediately sent out five Igorot runners and some Americans, to comb the hills and winding trails.

The search was thus continued every day for a week—but in vain. It is possible that Sister followed a group along a side trail!

In the camp at Muntinlupa, where she was recuperating from her Los Baños experience, Sister Constance heard of Sister Hyacinth's disappearance. Immediately, she with Sister Fidelis, and with the aid of American soldiers, but contrary to their advice, went to the hills. Baguio had not been delivered. It was a perilous trip, but Sister Constance wished to be at hand *when* Sister Hyacinth, her gentle companion of eighteen years, was found. For a long time, mindful of that Loss on the road from Jerusalem, two thousand years ago, Maryknollers hoped that Sister Hyacinth might be discovered in some hidden tribal village teaching and instructing! But her pattern must have been completed.

* * * *

An editorial in the New York Herald Tribune for February 28, 1945, reads in part:

General MacArthur has ordered southwest Pacific campaign service ribbons distributed to the civilian internees released by his troops in the Philippines—a graceful and merited tribute to American fortitude and endurance that the wrath of the foe could not break.

In days of hectic activity and heroic deeds, when millions post o'er land and ocean, or "slip the surly bonds of earth, dancing the skies on laughter silvered wings," it is a wholesome thought that they also serve who wait and suffer.

PART TWO

China

6

The Rock

HONG KONG proper is a mountain island set in a great bay, designed by Nature and developed by man as one of the great harbors of the world. The mountain is inhabited on all levels, from the bund to the peak. Not only for the tourist but for all beauty lovers, one of the captivating night sights is this huge rock, lighted through the wizardry of electricity, glowing and scintillating and reflecting herself almost endlessly in the depths of the sea. Even the most tender of social consciences is lulled temporarily, and the hidden cankers of squalor and ignorance and superstition are forgotten.

An extension of Hong Kong is Kowloon, across the bay, on the China mainland. Here the great ocean liners dock; through here, much of the wealth of the East passes; here the fleet Clipper planes, successors to the old clipper sailing vessels, come to rest. The harbor has not yet been spanned by great steel arches, the hallmark of western modernity. Communication between the two sections of Great Britain's Crown Colony is by means of the fussy little Kowloon Star ferry boat. Old timers recall a song partly in praise and partly in jeer of this sole and unreliable vehicle of water transportation.

Kowloon, in 1921, was made the center for the newly-arrived Maryknoll Sisters. In time, the Sisters went into the provinces, and now cover a goodly portion of the untilled vineyard which is pagan South China. Kowloon remained procurator headquarters. Here, too, the Sisters developed other works—educational, catechetical, industrial. In 1937, the Kowloon Community moved into its new Maryknoll Convent School—"the most artistic modern structure, harmonious with its Eastern surroundings, outside of Peiping" someone said of it, and functional as well. The building which dominates a high terrace is of brick, in tones of tan and ivory, with a high pitched, gable roof, covered with tiles of lovely Chinese blue, and built around a quadrangle. For years the Sisters had operated two schools, one on the mainland, the other in Hong Kong. When the attack was launched, there were Maryknoll Sisters in both sectors of the Colony.

Hong Kong, geographically, geologically, and from the point of view of military fortifications, was in a stronger position than was Kowloon. Too, in Kowloon there were located the docks, the air fields, the electric light plant, and the godowns for such vital war materials as the oil stations at nearby *Lai Chi Kok,* and the dynamite depots at Stonecutter's Island, a military post. If it were not written in their strategy, at any rate, the Japanese bombed with almost perfect precision these important objectives, and were in Kowloon ten days before the capitulation of Hong Kong.

News of the attack at Pearl Harbor had not reached the Maryknoll Sisters in Hong Kong and Kowloon. Their first intimation of actual conflict came when the great silver bombers swooped from the heavens and with unerring accuracy fired the docks and destroyed the American Clipper, which like a giant sea gull had settled on the waters of Hong Kong Bay the evening before. From it, eight newly fledged Maryknoll priests had stepped ashore. They came almost as sacrificial offerings to the holocaust of war. In the days that followed they were spared nothing of the horrors except actual death:—torture, threat, the sight of fellow beings led off, the sound of shots, the shrill cry that bespoke the bayonet.

The British Government had planned for the event of an attack. Blackout regulations and air raid practice were in force as early as September 1939. First Aid stations were organized, auxiliary nurses were trained, hospitals were alerted. But war was hard to conceive under a tropical sun that makes for dalliance and a mind-set that considers the white man's supremacy as a biological certainty.

The first wave of bombers changed the Maryknoll School into a military First Aid station. Doctors and nurses reported promptly, but the ambulance service broke down. The carts and lorries engaged for this work never arrived. Some had been caught on the wrong side of the blownup bridges—for the British immediately destroyed the roadways from the New Territories; others undoubtedly were used by persons fleeing from the danger zone. For five days, Kowloon was bombed and shelled. Enemy planes again and again encircled the convent, as they tried to get a British anti-aircraft gun set up at the end of Waterloo Road. Once they scored a hit—on the school. The actual shattering of glass and rending of brick and mortar and plaster are not so frightening as the peculiar whine of a descending bomb.

On the first day, while there was still freedom of action for those who scorned dropping bombs, Maryknoll's Father Feeney caught one of the last ferries from the Rock to the mainland, and established himself nominally as official chaplain to the Sisters. In the troubled months that followed, he became all things to the besieged group, for on December 12th the Japanese invaded the Convent. From that fateful day to February 8, 1942, when the Kowloon Sisters were interned in Stanley Jail, they were virtually prisoners in the lower reaches of their building. At night Father quietly placed his cot across the outside entrance to the Sisters' section; when interviews were demanded Father accompanied the Sisters in charge and sat in on the conferences; when searches and inspections were in order he was with the Sisters who showed the way. And in the comparative quiet of the morning he brought Christ down upon the Altar, communicated Him as Food and strength, and kept Him sacramentally dwelling among men.

Kowloon fell on December 12th; according to Sister Regina on that day at 2:30, Dr. Selwyn Clark, Director of Medical Services in Hong Kong, accompanied by Dr. Finelly, gave orders to disband our post and to send all the auxiliary nurses and all the women in the house to La Salle College—which had a larger Red Cross staff, including foreign men.

Dr. Clark urged that the Sisters also be evacuated to La Salle College. Sister Paul decided to remain in residence but to send to La Salle the youngest Sisters and those who were not well, a move which she later rued.

So soon as the status of the Convent changed from that of a Government First Aid Post, friends and refugees flocked in. Because of its construction, the building was one of the safest in the Colony.

In advance of the invading army, those who could moved over to Hong Kong. Kowloon presented a triple danger—the presence of the enemy, the activity of Chinese looters, the failure of communication. The British, as they withdrew, did the routine destruction of retreat, wrecked the electric light and telephone plants, and sank everything afloat in the harbor.

Possession may be nine-tenths of the law, but Sister Paul's decision to remain at the convent proved that even when lawlessness is rampant, tenure of place is a telling argument. At five o'clock the evening of Friday, December 12, 1941, three Japanese officers, with a Christian Brother and a Doctor, came over from La Salle College, where the Japanese were already installed. The officers demanded quarters and supplies—sheets, bedding, towels and face cloths for two hundred. They selected the auditorium and two classrooms on the south side for their use. But before long, the entire building, except the basement section where the Sisters lived, was occupied by the invaders.

It was about six-thirty that evening that the conquering army entered Kowloon. The Japanese came in tanks—except for the grinding tread of the caterpillars, they seemed like lumbering trees, so camouflaged were they with green boughs; they came in lorries, squatting or kneeling, helmets and uniforms covered with waving branches, little men tensely alert, with guns in position, bayonets drawn.

"Birnam wood do come to Dunsinane"

Up and down the streets the cars rolled, driven by men certainly not unfamiliar with the layout of the town! Sister Regina relates:

We picked up a bit for supper and lay in darkness behind locked doors. Throughout the night, we heard the Japanese marching with steady tread and in grim silence. Tanks and motor lorries altered the cadence, but never a human voice. The sounds coming out of the darkness gave the uncomfortable suggestion of something uncanny, implacable, relentless, grim. We could not sleep.

Early Friday morning, December twelfth, Fathers Feeney, Donnelly, and Sullivan said their Masses in the tiffin room with a congregation of about fifty. The tiny flame of the candles in the blacked-out room, the murmured prayers of the Chinese, the whimpering of the babies, made us think of the catacombs, and with fervor, we prayed for protection and help.

The bombing of Kowloon had ceased, but the shelling from Hong Kong increased. The attack on the Rock itself mounted in fury. There was the constant thunder of guns, the angry bark of planes, the whistle of dropping bombs, the roar of explosions. There was concern for the fate of the Sisters in Hong Kong; there was deep sympathy for the suffering; there was above all the sense of frustration in that the services of charity to the needy were limited to a single house!

Sister Paul had put in food supplies against a day of need. She had bought for the industrial department lovely materials, silks and brocades and delicate linens to be wrought into vestments and altar adornings, by the native girls who thus earned a livelihood. The foodstuffs had to be moved nearer to the point of ultimate consumption. The wealth of the looms of Cathay had to be concealed in an attic recess. Wasted energy this latter proved to be. Months later, when Sister Paul obtained her release from Stanley Internment Camp and managed on a business pretext to get into her one-time school, she was received by the presiding officer. He sat at what had been her desk, and across it, as a throw, was a piece of the precious cloth of gold with a burn from a cigarette in it! In the streets, Sister was to see soldiers strutting about, wearing shirts in strictly liturgical hues—red, green, purple, or decked out in fine linen, the loot from the Convent!

The first communication with the Japanese offered linguistic difficulties according to Sister Regina.

> Our interview had to be carried on in Chinese—the characters are the same in both languages. We feared there might be some misunderstandings, so we sent for Sister Famula at La Salle, who had been in Dairen for six years and spoke Japanese. Although it had been four years since Sister had used the language, we were relieved to find she was able to converse fluently. From then on, our dealings with the invaders were swathed in all the polite forms so dear to Orientals, and the results were far happier than they might have been if we had not had our providential interpreter.

Sister Famula is a sportswoman after the fashion of her blue grass Kentucky. She knows horses and loves a handicap. There was a challenge in her position as interpreter that put her on her mettle. Sister Paul in all her contacts with the Japanese took the position of one "also subject to authority." Her personality combined with cool confidence, and a clear knowledge of ends she wanted to attain, stood her in good stead while a prisoner in her own house, in internment camp, and later in Hong Kong. Sister's fearless demands, expressed by Sister Famula in the courtesy of the best Japanese tradition, were usually accepted as right and fitting. The brusque orders of war lords, especially when delivered with drawn bayonets, lost much of their terror and some of their dignity when construed in easy Americanese.

The officers were usually friendly. Almost nightly, there would be a tap on the door, which announced callers. Sister Famula, with Sister Paul or Sister Regina, and Father Feeney would go forth from the shelter. These absences caused concern to those left behind, but invariably the Sisters would report an hour spent in discussing the relative merits of various Shoyu sauce recipes; or hearing about the folks back home in Japan; or listening to accounts of great Japanese victories—fortunately the Sisters classified these as tall stories! One enterprising chap took an English lesson daily. He brought to Sister Famula copies of signs seen in the town. Keeping a poker face, Sister would translate "Peninsula Hotel," "Drink Two Beers," "No Parking." As regular as the lesson, on his departure, the soldier would make a stiff bow and present Sister with a chocolate bar.

There were times when the soldiers were strictly on business bent. Sister Regina describes one such incident.

A detachment of soldiers peremptorily asked to see the one hundred and twenty Japanese women who, they had heard, were interned on our compound. When we assured them that no Japanese women were on the precincts, they demanded to search the place. With bayonets drawn, they formed a procession: Sister Paul with a soldier guard; Sister Famula likewise escorted; Sister Regina with military attendants; Father Feeney with his guard. It was mighty uncomfortable walking amidst gleaming points, borne by ferocious looking soldiers. It was even more terrifying for the Sisters who did not know what was going on, to have us march into their quarters thus accompanied. Not a room in the building but was inspected. Whenever a Sister stopped to lock a door, the guard drew in close. Nor was it reassuring, after this one grand tour, to hear the soldiers rehearse the exact location of every nook and cranny. But they were satisfied that we harbored no women of their country.

The story continues:

Each day had its full share of eventfulness, but of them all, December 22nd claimed undisputed preeminence, for it was on the Monday before Christmas, that seven hundred prisoners of war, British, Canadians, Hong Kong Volunteers and Indians, all in a deplorable condition, were lodged under our roof.

The soldiers were a sorry lot of sick and wounded, starved and famished men. For three days, they had not tasted food; for twenty-four hours, not a drop of water had slaked their thirst. Most of them had dysentery; some had shed so much blood that their clothes were as stiff as boards. Yet we were not allowed to minister to them.

Nor were the poor fellows to receive a meal that night! The next morning, Father Feeney was permitted to hear confessions and give Communion to about thirty Catholic lads. By noon, Sister Corazon, M.D., Sister Camillus, R.N., and Sister St. Dominic,

R.N. were admitted. While they were dressing the wounded and tending the very ill, a victrola blared out *Home Sweet Home*. For a moment, some of the men thought it an American's bad idea of a joke. The Japanese had brought an army truck in the driveway. It carried a victrola with a huge horn. Undoubtedly it was an effort to break down the morale of the foreigners. It only succeeded in making every one angry. By night the men had moved on to the permanent prison camp on Argylle Street.

The house called for some vigorous disinfecting. Some of the Sisters were overseeing the job, while in turn a guard watched them. Sister Matthew Marie gives the story:

One lovely blue sky morning, we were on the veranda about to disinfect some sections, when a shell whistled its way over one corner and buried itself in the neighbor's property. The Japanese officer on duty signalled "DOWN." He was as surprised as we were. Down we went—as flat as we could. When the officer rose to run, I followed at his heels. We were pals for the time being. Along the verandah we dashed, down the stairs clippety clop. On the first floor, he turned to the Japanese offices and I left him to rejoin my community. It was an English shell from Hong Kong—and the next one killed a horse!

Until February, when the Japanese took over the house as a hospital, the Convent School was but once without soldiers. The first troops were the engineers, men of refinement. The frequently changing personnel was in the social scale descending. There was one set whose duty according to Sister Regina

was to collect furniture, clothing, machinery, anything detachable from the surrounding homes, assemble it in our reception rooms, crate it, mark the box with a red cross, and get it off for Japan. One day, when Sister Paul was on reconnaissance duty, she was told she could take anything that was hers, and she knew better than try to fool them!

The group that pastured their horses on the lawn aroused the greatest ire in the Sisters. In South China a greensward is obtained and sustained at the price of hard labor and unrelenting vigilance. These animals not only brought a pest of flies, but they frolicked on the grass, nipped the scarlet bougainvillea blossoms, charged at the hibiscus bushes, crushed the pale gardenias, trampled the prized torch ginger plants, and—wrecked the precious vegetable garden where a tomato was showing promise. The Kentuckian made a considered judgment: "Horses? Nay, nags!"

Sister Paul regretted dispatching part of her family to La Salle. She had come to realize that the convent would be commandeered and when the move came, she wanted the family together. Moreover, La Salle was in the hands of the Japanese. The place was crowded. There were daily inquisitions and nightly scares. As a protective measure, the Christian Brothers organized groups of men to act as escorts for the Sisters and nurses on night duty. Sister Joseph Marie tells that

> One night there was great commotion in a ward. The Japanese guards, fully armed, with bayonets fixed, rounded up the nurses and herded them into the Matron's office. This office was just outside the library where we were. Those of us not on shift heard loud banging on the office door, then angry voices raised in questioning and accusation. The guards had seen flashlights and interpreted them as signals to the Hong Kong side. Each nurse was given a grilling examination and had her pockets searched. Then they were dispatched to the ward. Next morning, despite the explanations that the lights were used only in caring for the patients, they were collected. The apology for the uproar of the previous night did not compensate for the loss of the flashes.
>
> Heavy and continuous shelling was the order of the nights. Since the fall of Kowloon, the Japanese were trying to effect a landing in Hong Kong at the nearest point, which landing was Lai Moon Pass. La Salle College commands a good view of the harbor and Lai Moon Pass in particular, which is perhaps four miles from the College. The shelling began at dusk and continued throughout the night. From the College, we could see the burst of shells on the Kowloon side and watch the progress of the response from the Rock.

By Christmas, Sister Paul had her group intact once more, except for the five Sisters attached to Holy Spirit School, Hong Kong.

Since December 8th they had been on duty at Queen Mary's Hospital.

In normal times, this hospital was reserved for Government officials and employees and for Chinese patients. With the war and the difficulties of transportation, more and more of the military were brought in. The first few days of hostilities, things went slowly. The Japanese were concentrating upon Kowloon. When it fell, Hong Kong was in for special attention. For the first two weeks, however, the casualties were light, so the newspapers said, and the hospital staff agreed. Sister Amata, apropos of this, remarks: "I'm not an R.N.—just a school teacher turned into an auxiliary nurse, so I thought privately things were bad enough. But I lived and learned that Sherman knew war!"

Queen Mary Hospital is a short distance from Mt. Davis, one of the forts guarding the entrance to the harbor. From some of the wards personnel and patients could watch the men operate the guns, but likewise could they see the enemy bombs and shells explode on the fort with devastating results. Certainly the view was not any more conducive to recovery than were the noises. Sister continues:

> The next few weeks are blurred in my memory. It now seems like a continual shrieking of air raid signals, of guns blasting, of shells whistling and whining, of machine guns spitting, of planes soaring and diving with the aftermath of exploding bombs and of endless streams of bleeding humanity. Usually they were unconscious, but quiet, determined, self-controlled, when they were conscious.
>
> The Chinese nurses were grand, worked well and were cooperative. I think the Chinese are born democrats—I'm not talking about politics but natural tendencies. The English nurses were composed, capable, magnificent, but even in this hour of sifting, they maintained an attitude of insular aloofness.

Two Jesuit priests and a Chinese scholastic were assigned to duty at Queen Mary Hospital.

> All during our stay at the hospital, we had two Masses each morning in a Doctor's office. It was gratifying to see how many

availed themselves of the opportunity to take part. Masses were arranged so that the group going on duty could attend the first Mass, and the night nurses the second. We were on eight hour duty.

Christmas Masses were crowded. Almost every Catholic received Holy Communion. . . . Many of the boys became daily communicants. Before they were transferred, I think all but one had received the Sacraments.

In a lull between the fusillades, Sister Maria Regis and Sister Amata scurried home to their Convent, for the first time, to collect everything that might make for a happier celebration for the sick. They escaped a spray of shrapnel when a bomb hit a nearby hill. On the way back to the hospital they got a lift in a lorry filled with Canadian soldiers. The boys were cheery, put the Sisters in the midst of them, and sat with guns in their hands. They went out of their way to deposit the Sisters safely at the hospital. Later the Sisters learned of whole lorries of these youths being wiped out by hand grenades. Sister Amata takes up her story:

We got back to the Hospital in time to go on duty. I glanced from the window as I walked down the ward to "scrub up." Slowly, very slowly, the white flag was going up on the fort across the way. A soldier stood in the road with a huge white flag. Others were carrying out guns and ammunition and placing them on the lawn. I walked out on the verandah for air! Above me, a Royal Scot whistled softly *God Save the King*. Down in the next ward a little Cockney hummed *There'll Always Be An England*.

The Rock had fallen. And that morning the British paper had reported the situation well in hand! It was. But the hand was Japanese!

It was a Christmas of contrasts, a day of light and shadow, a song of love and a hymn of hate; the Babe of Peace and *The Veteran of Heaven*:

O Captain of the wars, whence won Ye so great scars?
  In what fight did Ye smite, and what manner was the foe?
Was it on a day of rout they compassed Thee about,
  Or gat Ye these adornings when Ye wrought their overthrow?

' 'Twas on a day of rout they girded Me about,
They wounded all My brow, and they smote Me through the side;
My hand held no sword when I met their armed horde,
And the conqueror fell down, and the Conquered bruised his pride.'

What is *Thy* Name? Oh, show!—'My Name ye may not know;
'Tis a going forth with banners, and a baring of much swords;
But My titles that are high, are they not upon My thigh?
"King of Kings!" are the words, "Lord of Lords!";
It is written "King of Kings, Lord of Lords." ' *

The Hong Kong garrison was interned immediately upon the surrender. Civilians went unmolested for a week. The evacuation of the hospital patients took place on January 20th. Sister Amata records:

It was a warm winter morning, lit by pale sunlight, which seemed to touch gently the scars of the city.

Every one was to go—regardless of condition, splints, casts, unconsciousness. We were so concerned about the patients that I don't think the staff gave any thought to their newly acquired status as civilian internees.

Large trucks were brought in front of the hospital and the patients were loaded in. One Canadian lad had just had his eye removed, and while he was still under the anaesthetic, I rolled him down to the unpadded, springless car. He had false teeth, which had been removed before the operation. I was afraid that they might be lost, so I wrapped them in a piece of gauze, which I pinned to his gown. Just in case any attendant might think the bag held money, I took time out to show the teeth all round. In lifting him to the truck, the blankets had come undone and I knew it would be dangerous should he get a chill. I was in a quandary. We had been instructed by the British Hospital authorities to make a "scrounge" and take what supplies we could into internment. My mantle, therefore, was the receptacle for many things, personal and otherwise. If I put the cape down on the ground, the curious guards would be sure to do a thorough inspection. So I walked up to the sentry, pushed aside his bayonet, and thrust my mantle into his hands, motioning him to mind

* Francis Thompson: "The Veteran of Heaven," *Poems of Francis Thompson,* Oxford.

it. An officer came over to intervene. I had noted that the truck was high, and though I knew I could make the leap, despite my long skirts, I had an idea it might be too conspicuous. Assuming that my dealing with the sentry was just in the ordinary routine of his life, I gently guided the officer to the lorry, and used his shoulder as a prop to clamber aboard the car. I covered up the patient. The Japanese officer waited and offered his shoulder in my descent. We bowed deeply, gravely to each other; I retrieved my belongings from the sentry, bowed to him, and decamped. I didn't see the funny side until much later.

The next day the Queen Mary staff was on the way to Stanley Jail for internment. The Maryknoll Fathers had been moved there the day previous. At the end of the month, and almost without notice, the La Salle staff of British doctors, nurses and aides, two American Christian Brothers, and a group of Canadians were transported to the prison. The handwriting on the wall was clear for all to read.

Sister Paul hoped for the best and prepared for the worst. Through the kindness of the Italian Fathers, she was able to store some valuables with them. Each Sister kept a bag packed for an emergency move. When February 8, 1942, arrived, the Sisters had about decided they were to remain in their own building for the duration. After Mass, but before the morning coffee, word was received that not only the day had arrived, but that the hour approached. Eleven A. M. was set.

Sister Paul with Sister Famula immediately appeared at Japanese Headquarters to ask not only for an extension of time but for a truck to carry the baggage! Both requests were granted! Upon which, each internee added a mattress to her equipment, and enfolded within it, a duffle bag of food. It is safe to say that throughout the various shiftings necessitated by being enemies in a foreign land, the Sisters rolled up an all-American record as luggage carriers.

In the meleé of packing, Bishop Valtorta arrived. He was keenly distressed, for he had made every effort to have the priests and the Sisters interned in their own houses.

It was a raw, drear, wet day, such as South China offers for winter weather. The first half of the departants, with the Brothers, rode to the ferry on the truck and in a small car, accompanied by a Japanese officer. At the wharf, humans and goods and chattels were transferred to the sidewalk. While the truck returned for a second load, the baggage was put aboard a small launch, arranged for by the officer. It was the lot of the second group to say the last goodbye and leave in the almost forsaken convent, the little group of Third Nationals not included in the internment orders, a Chinese, three Portuguese, a Filipina. How long they would be permitted to remain in the convent, no one knew. Fears were hid neath smiles, tears neath laughter:

> If men ask ye why ye smile and sorrow
> Tell them ye grieve, for your hearts know Today,
> Tell them ye smile, for your eyes know Tomorrow.

When these Sisters discovered sentries posted at their convent doors on the morning of February 12th, they knew that dispossession was a matter of but a short time.

The guards had been instructed not to allow anything to be removed from the building. The Japanese wanted a furnished house. At first these watchmen were definitely unbending, but Father Feeney, in a few days, made friends with them, one of whom was to prove particularly helpful. Father's little kindnesses—a cigarette, a cup of tea, a thermos put on the door step at night with a hot drink—were prompted not by any guile, but by his concern for all humanity. Thoughtfulness pays dividends.

On February 14th the Sisters were told to move. They protested they had no place to go. The available houses were shambles, electric and plumbing fixtures gone, window frames and doors, even staircases ripped out for kindling wood. So the Sisters tarried. On the 19th, a Japanese major in charge of hospital affairs called and informed the household that it would have to be cleared out by the following afternoon. Nor was he open to argument or reason, as to day or hour. He did promise to supply a truck—not a great comfort when one has no fixed destination.

Then a Chinese doctor living in a flat across the street agreed to let his apartment go to the Sisters. Pictures of disconsolate religious perched atop a table on a street corner vanished. But more important, here was a flat, with families living all around and located right next to the parish house.

The next morning the faithful Christian Brothers who had lost their all, relatives and friends of the Sisters, rallied round for the last move only to be sternly denied entrance to the compound. Then it was that Father Feeney's watchman took on importance. He wrote a note, directed Father where to take it, and Father returned with a permit for the multitude to pour into the convent. The evening before, this guard had tried to express his sympathy to Father—he took a small English-Chinese-Japanese dictionary and pointed out the words—Sentence (judgment)—remove—heart—wail—suffering—sorrow—sorry—like—lightning—peace. Sister Candida Maria relates how

> the truck failed to appear at nine-thirty as promised. In the meantime, Dr. N., a military officer who had always been friendly, came for his sixth inspection in ten days. I told him our troubles. He called a sentinel—that morning they were as plentiful as flies around sugar, gave commands, and in a very short time the car appeared. While I was going through the house with the Doctor, Father Feeney called out cheerfully, "Don't hurry, Sister, keep him as long as you can. We'll do the moving." I'll never know if the Doctor understood the message. He spoke English, but slowly. I looked at him, and could read nothing in his imperturbable countenance. He was looking over records—which had been ours—and continued to discuss the merits of *Il Trovatore, Aida, La Traviata,* and *Carmen.*

Sister Cecilia Marie writes of the last quarter-hour at Maryknoll Convent School. They were typically human, one grasps at small things in historic moments!

> Towards one o'clock and after the departure of the Major, a petty officer came in and refused to allow us to move any more furniture. We had saved what we could. Bread was baking in the

oven and the dinner was cooking on the stove. With steaming dinner in hands, and our two dogs on leash, we walked to our new home.

It was in this small flat, in the shadow of their own lovely convent, that Sister Paul met the five when after two months she and three other Sisters were released from Stanley. Later when Holy Spirit School was vacated and found to be habitable, Sister Paul made it headquarters for the community. The location was more accessible, for buses were few and crowded and slow. It was there that the second group went from camp, and it was from there that the Sisters started on their various ways into the interior.

* * * *

The Chinese did not fare well in Hong Kong. They saw nothing of the *co*-prosperity promised, nor did they seek it. The *New Order* was cruel and harsh. The Chinese were not interned —but forced into exile. The Imperial command was that 400,000 leave the colony. This order was enforced by the simple expedient of stopping the sale of rice. Each person who left was given a pint of rice for food on the way. At the rate of ten thousand a day, they trudged out the Castle Peak Road to Shumshun and into—not a land of plenty, but a war-worn, drought-stricken country. Gracious women and beautiful girls replaced their colorful brocades with the shabby *shaam* of the peasant; they hid their ornaments of green and cream colored jade, of lapis lazuli, of pearl; their peach blossom skins, they streaked with ashes; their delicate hands they tried to make look rough. If so disguised, they escaped the attention of the enemy, if they had homes or relatives in the country, if they were stout walkers, if they eluded the bandits, who had a mushroom growth, then only were they comparatively safe. The poor, and they were legion, faced starvation. In the interior of China, died countless thousands, victims of the expulsion from Hong Kong.

When the excess population was thus eliminated, the Japanese opened a rice market. Buyers formed a line five abreast, under the vigilant eyes of the police. The queue might stretch out for a quarter of a mile. Each person was permitted to purchase one *kattie*—in English measure about a pound and a third—enough to feed a single person for one day. The housewife might not buy for her family. At the snail's pace at which the line moved, people often remained through the night in order to have a place in the morning.

Of the Chinese represented in the Victory Parade, there were several classes. Some men honestly believed that the rule of the white man should end. And certainly it must undergo a radical change. These men aligned themselves on the side of the New Order and worked with, and under, the Japanese. Their good intent may not be challenged. So many of this number were to resign and leave the Colony, that the Japanese finally refused to accept resignations from those useful to them, or from those who knew too much; neither would they issue travel permits to them or to their families. There was a second group of time-servers, not indigenous to any one country, whose interest is pure self-interest. The third class, and by far the largest, consisted of the poor and hungry, who marched just for a day's pay—three kattie of rice. Sister Clement says of this group:

> I had always thought that, for a town of its size, Hong Kong had a goodly proportion of that pathetic class of people to whom one's heart goes out in deepest sympathy, the poor and destitute, but now they had increased and multiplied. We saw, the day after our release from Stanley, on one corner, a poor woman crying from hunger and eating some scraps she had salvaged from the garbage pile. A little further on, two men, too weak to stand, were lying in the street crying piteously for help. So it was all along the way; and we could see these poor outcasts, growing weaker and more emaciated, day by day. Then there came a day when the streets were rid of these unfortunates. There was ugly black talk of a boat ride. We do not know the truth! but this is certain, the New Order does not believe that Blessed are the poor.

There was a class of the 'new poor' in Hong Kong, people who had enjoyed wealth, or at least comforts. These perhaps were the greater sufferers, for their rearing had not prepared them for stark hunger and biting cold.

Wood was a great problem for the people. They were forbidden to cut it on the hillsides and prices were exorbitant. Often we heard a commotion in the street caused by a policeman slapping a woman because she had gathered a miserable bundle of firewood to cook her rice. . . . Slapping was quite a popular form of immediate chastisement. Sometimes the dangerous dogs were allowed to mete out—injustice.

The social and economic destruction wrought in Hong Kong and Kowloon by the war the Sisters had some opportunity to survey between their release from camp and their departure for the interior. The diarist writes:

While in camp, we were deeply grateful to Dr. Selwyn Clarke for his excellent work in behalf of the sick and his efforts to relieve anxiety. . . . Once out of camp, I soon learned that his field of good works extended to the non-British wives and families of military prisoners. He accepted our offer to help visit these people and report to him their needs.

In visiting some of these families in Wanchai districts, I had an opportunity to see the effects of the war. Whole blocks of buildings had been bombed, shelled, and then demolished by the looters. One family we found on the second floor of one of these shells of buildings. The place was completely bare of furniture, except for a couple of boards for beds which were to take care of two young wives with several children each, and the mother of one of them—and the mother of a young woman is old in China! The absence of doors and windows, and some side walls, gave them the open-air life, summer and winter. These young women, whose husbands are in camp, were quite typical of the others we visited, patiently bearing their hardships, asking for nothing, but so deeply grateful for the least thing done for them—even only a word of sympathetic interest. I was impressed, too, by the friendly, helpful attitude of the people. For example, one little mother, with her child on her back walked a long way with us to be sure we found the address we were looking for. And remember, walking on an empty stomach calls for quiet heroism.

So far as the invaders were concerned, the English language would be obliterated from the Colony according to Sister Clement:

All the streets were given Japanese names. The English signs were removed or painted over, or chipped out. There were two buses that started from the same point—one went toward St. Paul's and beyond, the other branched off to Happy Valley. The signs were characters, one in black on a white background, the other in white on a black background. I didn't know the characters, and I couldn't remember the color scheme—so bus riding from that point held for me a strong element of chance. When schools opened late in the spring of 1942, English was forbidden.

The only people who got any kind of a chance in Hong Kong were the children. The Japanese have a real love for them, and the little ones responded. It was not an uncommon sight, and it stirred up the ashes of one's hope for a future peace based on friendship of all peoples to see children and the army of occupation walking hand in hand, or skating in the streets of the fallen city. Sister Clement's narrative continues:

The high cost of living was frightening. Flour that had cost $6.00 per bag before the war was now, when sold under government control, $70.00, and in the flourishing black market, it was $200.00 per bag. Carnation milk was $10.00 per tin, and milk in China comes only in a can! Beef was $14.00 per pound. Flour and sugar were rationed by the Government. The sugar allowance was about one pound per month per person. Gas and light had gone up five times their former price, and there was a fixed minimum fee for light regardless of consumption.

The enemy national banks were allowed to pay $500.00 against each deposit. Twenty percent of the balance was allowed to be drawn later, but what was this with prices at such a level. In the early days of the occupation, the military yen was put in circulation, with an exchange of two dollars Hong Kong to one dollar military yen. In July the rate was fixed at four dollars Hong Kong to one dollar military yen, and all government bills, taxes, light, gas, and water, had to be paid in military yen. This necessitated another endless line. Business was poor. Shopkeepers opened for short hours, some of them claimed, under compulsion. Foreign business firms had to submit statements of their accounts, and were permitted to draw only their running expenses. Property owners suffered. Rents were fixed by the government at a low rate and the property was taxed at a very high one. Most of the owners found it impossible to cover the expenses of the upkeep of their property. We knew one man who had an entire block of houses confiscated without any compensation. On the other hand, there were instances where houses were commandeered by the Army men without the knowledge of the government; sometimes a proper presentation of the case brought about a readjustment.

There were incidents which ranged from the merely annoying to the tragic. At points a sentry might call all foreigners out of a bus, make them bow to him, submit to search if he so ordered—but the most aggravating part of the procedure consisted in the fact that the soldiery took the seats thus emptied. One little old Chinese lady demanded her seat so insistently that the incumbent yielded!

There was the ceremony at all public buildings where passers-by had to bow ceremoniously to the guard. On entering such august precincts, one had to wash one's hands in an antiseptic and wipe one's feet on a mat saturated with a like solution. Along the bus routes were stations where passengers were searched—person and baggage; and there was a like set-up on the ferry. Usually the Sisters were exempt.

People were still leaving Hong Kong a year after the battle. Maryknoll friends, old and new, were among the "departants." Every day there were good-byes to say, writes Sister Clement.

All felt it was useless to remain and were seeking their livelihood elsewhere. It grieved us to see so many of our girls in such reduced circumstances, but there was a gratifying side, too. The war and its consequences had brought out in many a spoiled darling strong qualities, giving them the realization of spiritual values and Christian principles that we often feared we had but cast upon the waters. It had taken long years, and hard sailing—even here was reward exceeding great.

Sister Paul was sending her Sisters into the interior two by two as the opportunity could be *made*. It was not always easy to do. One might be passed and the other held up. There were twin dangers—bullets and brigands. But all got through safely. The shadow still lay on the Rock. There was good work afield and Maryknoll would return to Hong Kong!

7

Bread and Barbed Wire

"LADY" or "bread giver" was the title awarded Sister Gonzaga in the internment camp at Stanley. There bread was always a problem, hunger an ever present specter. The menu was invariable. Come Sunday, come Monday, January or March, there was wormy rice, with a thin sort of fish stew or gravy in the morning; in the evening, there was a thin sort of fish stew or gravy with wormy rice. Then in April a bag of flour was given the Maryknoll Fathers to be shared with the Sisters. When the gift was delivered, Father Meyer had added a cake of yeast which, with typical foresight, he had salvaged from the Maryknoll Procure the day the priests were confined. Sister Gonzaga made bread like Mother used to bake and as a thank you, she sent a loaf to the founder of the feast. The next day the donor called to make a business proposition—he would supply flour if Sister would make the bread. Her problem became not flour but yeast. She had saved part of the original cake. Her efforts to grow it in rice failed. Then she procured sweet potato *peelings* from the communal kitchen and, scraping them, she obtained enough substance to boil. This proved a good base for the yeast. Thereafter the baker had a priority over fifty others for the use of the small stove in their section.

Sister lived up to her title "lady" to the full extent of Ruskin's demand that the bread be not only for the household but broken among the multitude! In the block occupied by the American bachelors there was an old sailor, Mr. Gingles, a retired naval chief steward, a one-time restaurateur in Hong Kong, and now cook for the men. Mr. Gingles had some one ask Sister to show him the yeast secret. Sister was delighted to share the results of her little experiment. From that time sweet potatoes were assured, as Mr. Gingles sent them with sugar and his compliments until their liberation. In *The Saturday Evening Post* for January 9th and 16th, under the caption, *Starvation is Torture Too,* Mr. Joseph Alsop, newsman, gives a picturesque description of the ex-naval chef and lavishes upon him well-earned praise. He worked

Miracles with second grade rice and scrag ends of buffalo. His language was sulphurous and his formal education had been brief, but he had courage, leadership, humor, and an old-fashioned faith in people that put the faint hearts to shame. He kept us in good health and good heart. Although there were others among us who had occupied far more important positions in the outside world, Ed Gingles—for that was his remarkable name—became the accepted chieftain of our house.

There was an interim of about a week between the fall of Hong Kong and the internment of civilians. This period was spent by some people in trying to decide what a camper's outfit should be. In doubt, some elected—cigarettes—but most candidates decided in favor of a canned-food reserve and bedding.

The first place for civilian confinement was in the lowest section of the city, in so-called hotels, which were in reality old places of disrepute. The very existence of such ancient, dilapidated, dirty dens of evil was a crime for any government to countenance. Was it not "Mrs. Miniver" who regretted that war was necessary in order to teach just such plain, fundamental things as—painting a kerb white, taking city slum children to the country for a vacation? One might add developing some housing projects. This temporary camp lasted for seventeen days when the internees, probably about thirty-five hundred, in all, were moved to Stanley.

Stanley Peninsula is a narrow, hilly, barren neck of land, lying between two beautiful bays, with a vista beyond of high bluish green hills where the spacious homes of some of the internees stood. The tip of the Peninsula is a highland on which is located Stanley Fort. Here was the hardest fighting in the Battle of Hong Kong; here on that Christmas Day took place the atrocities so frequently noted. The Hong Kong Jail was at the end of the neck, with wardens' quarters, and administrative buildings. Nearby was St. Stephen's College with its faculty (or masters') houses. The houses, architecturally nondescript, in stucco finish, were solidly built and the plumbing had withstood the bombardment. The area covered roughly a square mile, entirely enclosed by barbed wire. The Carmel Cloister was just outside the 'enclosure' and the Maryknoll Fathers' House not distant. Sister Amata describes the advent of the first Maryknoll Sisters:

On January 21, 1942, the personnel from Queen Mary Hospital was sent to Stanley Jail. The matron told us to take whatever we needed from the hospital stock. Through this kindness, we, who had no possessions save the emergency bag we carried in with us, were well supplied. The lorry was piled high with our things and those of some English nurses. We all climbed up on top and were roped on with the baggage. The Maryknoll Fathers were 'in residence' at Stanley, since the previous day. They gave us a rousing welcome.

The five of us were shown to a room, where we unfolded our cots and started to set up light house-keeping. Father Meyer was soon knocking at our door with a basket of food—rice, a little meat, and vegetables. Our address was Roosevelt Avenue, but we lacked postal service!

The Americans were housed in three blocks, six apartments to a block, each apartment consisting of three rooms, a kitchenette and pantry, two servants' rooms, and a small laundry. Sixteen unassorted persons were put in each three rooms, two in each servant's room, and usually two in the kitchenette. These were Park Avenue suites in comparison with other quarters. The Bachelors' Club, membership of about fifty, was lodged on the second floor of a former clubhouse. The hall on the first floor was used for general assemblies and for religious services. The Japanese never used the prison itself for the internees, although many would gladly have occupied a cell for the sake of privacy, not possible in assigned quarters. And undoubtedly the British drew the poorest accommodations.

The men had already done a good job cleaning up the signs of carnage. The Fathers had contrived a large stove in one of the garages, which became the kitchen for the American group. The crew of a merchant marine, caught in Hong Kong for repairs, volunteered to do the cooking. It was a big order, even at two meals a day, for we numbered some two hundred and fifty, and they had to cook on a makeshift stove with less than a minimum of equipment and a modicum of food. With a degree of regularity, they publicly resigned at one of the general meetings because of criticism, but a vote of confidence restored their good name, and they would return to the job.

Then on February 8th, a rainy drizzly Sunday, we were given the news that the Kowloon Sisters had come. When we looked down and saw a huge lorry piled sky high and a bus full of Sisters, we knew that it was true! It was a happy reunion after a complete separation of three months—and such months.

After boarding about in the British quarters for some weeks, the Sisters were assigned to one of the "de luxe" apartments—thanks to the graciousness of Mr. Bill Hunt and the American camp executives. Sister Regina gives details of the set-up:

The room nearest the entrance was used as our main room. There was a table there and when it bore a white cloth, snowy, no matter how meager the meal and poor the service, this was our refectory. We ate buffet. Chairs numbered three, but boards on wooden trestles provided seats. We tried to think there was something monastic about it!

The same room was used as recreation, reception, and classrooms; music studio for Father Allie's choir; meeting place for the Catholic Action groups; and by night, dormitory for six Sisters. Three French windows gave it a nice appearance and deprived it of any privacy.

Our building possessed a hot water boiler, tended faithfully by Captain Miller, American. During the entire stay in camp, he supplied boiled water for drinking purposes to the American community and to some of his British friends. This service was a big factor in preventing disease.

The sanitary squad rivaled New York's White Wings, in the efficient manner they swept the streets, washed the gutters, gathered and buried the garbage.

The sandy soil, not the 'farmers,' must bear the burden of blame for the meager growth—limited mostly to some lettuce and carrots. The Peninsula most certainly was not a garden spot.

The Americans were taken care of by a Committee elected by themselves. Fairly regular assemblies were held, similar to the old fashioned *town meetin's,* where camp affairs were discussed openly, grievances aired, and usually cleared.

So the Sisters made their adjustments amid a poverty that was greater than they ever conceived when they had renounced all worldly possessions. In a materialistic era, in a land where the white man assumed a privileged position as by right divine, it was interesting to study the individual reactions of the civilian internees to changed conditions. Some persons merely shifted their sense of value to embrace, as worthwhile, objects of little cost and uncertain utility; others applied this same principle of acquisitiveness on a lower level, and seemed to thrive on a misconception of the truth: God helps those who help themselves; others again were heroic not only in accepting privations, but in extending a rich service to the needy—physical, psychological, spiritual. The majority ran the gamut between these extremes. While guards guarded the internees, the latter kept an eagle eye on their few but necessary possessions.

Camp rules touched the mere externals of existence. The Sisters established their 'way of life' and so not only participated in the communal life of the camp, but approximated as closely as possible the community life of their Congregation. This was a healthy and wholesome influence in the camp, and made for community solidarity, and personal holiness. It was to be the acid test of Mother Mary Joseph's considered judgment that the rule of the Maryknoll Sisters must be strong enough to link each member in a chain fastened at the Feet of Christ, and flexible enough to enable them to lead the full life under all trials and all circumstances.

There was prayer and study, cleaning and ironing, teaching and nursing. There was work in library and canteen. There were visits to make to the sick and lonely and religious instructions to give those who sought it. And there were the children. Sister Christella writes:

> Some of these young internees were such personalities. There was Michael, a fifteen year older, who was in the way of being a misfit. He was too advanced for the school, and too young to adjust himself philosophically to camp life. Some of the Sisters set his feet firmly on the road to Oxford. There was Deedee, aged two, who would waver into Father Meyer's Chinese class for the Sisters, mount the professorial knee and add his gibberish to ours. There was Vera, five years old, who feared no man nor beast. Where the crowd was thickest there was Vera; where food was to be found, there was Vera; where excitement ran highest, there was Vera—both cause and effect! There was Winnie, the only American girl left in camp after repatriation. At two, she was actively proving by example, word, and a slap or two when necessary, that American Independence was neither dead nor slumbering. Deedee was brother to Winnie. There was Leslie, friendly and smiling in an unfriendly world, but strong, too, and at three demonstrating that she wouldn't be overcome very easily. Then there was Danny of serious mien, with whom we felt a degree of comfort, for he often assured us the lions wouldn't eat the Sisters!

The presence of the missioners of every persuasion gave ample opportunity for each one to observe his or her religious practices. For Catholics, the Holy Sacrifice was offered daily in the three small chapels in camp. On Sunday morning there were three Masses in the assembly hall, and at each one there was an instruction on the Sacraments by one of the priests. This hall, in the afternoon, was given over to the Protestant denominations. However, in St. Stephen's Hall on the hill at three, there was Rosary, Benediction and a short discourse by Bishop O'Gara.

When Lent came to camp, there were Stations of the Cross. The question of Holy Week services came up, and the Bishop regretted that so many ceremonies would have to be omitted due to the scarcity of chapel equipment. So one Sunday morning, Sister Paul with Sister Maria Regis and Sister Famula took themselves to the prison to interview a Japanese official and to try to get permission to leave camp and visit Carmel! At long last, the passes were issued and a guard assigned. To anxious watchers it seemed they were gone aeons and their return in the later afternoon was hailed with delight. Sister Paul had not achieved all she set out to do, but she did bring back a monstrance, a cope, white chasuble, and dalmatics, some food from Mother Teresa's lean larder, and some fresh pears from *Japanese Headquarters!*

The Committee allowed the Catholics the use of the hall for Mass on Holy Thursday, Good Friday, and Holy Saturday. Thursday and Friday afternoons, services were held in St. Stephen's Hall. Solemn High Mass was sung by the Fathers on Easter Sunday. One of the Canadian Sisters, an artist, ingeniously contrived a mitre, even having semi-precious stones! The crozier was a gilded staff with a painted cardboard crook.

Holy Week was not observed with the full service or the splendor of a Cathedral, but the Crucified One must have looked in Love on His children as they sought and found strength in Him:

> But (when so sad thou canst not sadder)
> Cry;—and upon thy so sore loss
> Shall shine the traffic of Jacob's ladder
> Pitched betwixt Heaven and Charing Cross—

Or Stanley Prison. Alleluia!

Sister Frances Marion writes:

When we first went to camp the Immaculate Conception Sisters had already started a First Communion class so that the more advanced group received their First Holy Communion shortly after Easter. The date for the second group was set for sometime in May. The Immaculate Conception Sisters took care of providing in some way white dresses for the girls and suits for the boys. Bishop O'Gara asked us to take care of the Communion breakfast. The mothers of the children donated from their meager stores, a little sugar, a little cocoa, or a little flour. Then Sister Amata asked the Chairman of the British Committee for something for a party for the children. He appealed to the

Japanese on the hill and they sent down sugar, milk and cocoa. Mrs. McNeary, our neighbor in the block, who showed us extreme kindness on many an occasion, provided a large tin of orange marmalade. Sister Gonzaga made rolls. Sister Joseph Marie made cake which had chocolate frosting! None of the children had seen anything like *that* since they came into the camp. The morning of the Breakfast happened to be *one of the three* during our stay in camp when one egg was provided for each member of the community, so that all in all, we were able to give the children a really substantial breakfast. We cleared out our main room and by borrowing a table from another apartment were able to arrange a place for each of the twenty children. The tables were covered with sheets and decorated with greens. Bishop O'Gara sat at the head of the table completely at ease with his young friends, taking care of their various needs. One little girl at his left thoughtfully laid aside a piece of her bun and told him that it was for him! Even though the children had not seen a cake for many a day, nearly every child refrained from eating his or her piece. Instead each took it along to share with other members of the family!

Man does not live by bread alone! though of such importance is it that Christ Himself phrased the petition for sustenance of soul and body in the perfect prayer: *Give us this day our daily bread.*

Sister Paul accepted internment gracefully, but she never acceded to it as a state that could not and should not be changed. The Sisters in camp were organized; but in Kowloon, she had left five Sisters, and a building—in law the property of the Maryknoll Sisters, no matter what disposition was made of it by war. Throughout South China danger zones there were many others. From the beginning, Sister negotiated for her release. She would not endanger in any way her status as an American in which she gloried, but she would and did fall back on her Irish ancestry of which she was intensely proud. On April 21, 1942, Sister Paul led the first band back to Hong Kong—released on the grounds of their Irish forebears! On June the 5th a second group departed. For some time repatriation had been talked about. Sister Paul took this opportunity to return to the States ten Sisters—most of them for medical and surgical care; the rest for business reasons, looking forward to the rebuilding of the work. Sister Christella carries on the burden of the story until the end:

On a memorable Sunday, a letter came from Sister Paul listing those who were to remain. Hard lines on those to go . . .

But before departure Sister Paul visited camp to see her family; to take care of some business affairs for other internees; to wish Godspeed to Maryknollers taking to the seas. For her? She would get the Sisters out of Hong Kong into free China, and then she would visit the Sisters throughout the South. It took time, and much patience, and careful planning, and great endurance, and deep prayer—but she did!

When the Sisters sailed for home on the *Gripsholm,* June 29th, it was in the belief that the Sisters in camp would be released soon. September found all gone except two. Sisters Eucharista and Christella stayed to assist Father Meyer and Father Hessler in the instruction work. Voluntarily they remained almost a full year longer in captivity.

The exchange boat, according to camp rumor, was postponed and sunk numberless times, but on June 29th, the *Asama Maru* appeared on the horizon. We knew the parting was a reality.

From the cemetery, Stanley's highest point, we watched the repatriates, sharply silhouetted, move one by one along the pier, and as the ferry pulled away, we commended them to their Guardian Angels, prayed Him Who calmed the angry waters for their safe passage, and turned back to the one topsy-turvy room that was left us for headquarters.

We took up community life again—with its round of prayer and work—and it was good for us. . . .

The food rations issued by those in authority kept getting worse and worse and finally did not even approximate sustenance requirements. We received food from outside and so managed to exist. . . .

While I attempted to keep the home fires burning, Sister Eucharista struggled to impart a little religious knowledge to the children who attended school. Sister also manfully conducted the choir with good results. Along with this we kept the camp library. . . . Hospital visiting was part of our schedule. Good results were gained through the kindness of Father Meyer who spent his money buying eggs ($2.00 each) and distributing them freely to the needy patients, irrespective of race, color, religion or disposition, who had no means of getting extra food rations.

Chinese lessons with Father Meyer continued, so every morning we had an hour's session. The language usually became inextricably mixed up with fighting the war and winning the peace; in discourses on Catholic Action or arguments on the Liturgy; in discussions—deep and long—on how to improve the Johnny cake.

Christmas came to camp. The Sisters gave presents out of their poverty. Candy, and soap and the like, in gift packages—tin cans, covered with silver foil salvaged from cigarette packages.

Our remembrances, few and insignificant, were appreciated. One friend, reputed to have been the wealthiest woman in Hong Kong, shed tears of gratitude for the bar of soap we had slipped into her box!

The Infant for our Crib was cut out of a Sacred Heart Messenger and mounted on cardboard; the straw, weeds from the hillside.

Orders were given by the Japanese that Christmas trees might not be cut. If taken they must be lifted root intact and replaced after Christmas. Pines were all that grew in Stanley's sandy soil. Suddenly the boys developed deafness at an alarming rate, and their reading rating was on a moronic scale. The camp, including the Sisters' room, wore its evergreen with an air.

The place was in quarantine for diphtheria, so the Masses were offered out of doors. Christmas dinner was 'extra special'—the *pièce de résistance* being a few bits of pork wrapped in a cabbage leaf, and for dessert a slice of fruit cake for which the group had donated from supplies sent by the Red Cross.

It was interesting to note the difference between the Americans and the British in the greeting rendered. The "Merry Christmas" of the American internees was hearty, the factual British demanded—"why?"

New Year's dawned and on this day our English friends reciprocated with a "Happy New Year and a *happier* one next year."

Sister Paul had gotten the Sisters through to the interior. She herself was to leave. She would not allow us to remain longer behind barbed wire. On New Year's Day, Sister Eucharista and I signed papers that would permit us to go to Kwongchowan via Macao, "to return to Hong Kong never."

8

Bombs Away

"MAY the potencies of song and laughter abide with me ever." Joyousness is one of the outward signs of the inner grace of missioners. Storms cannot break it; sorrows cannot destroy it. The saga of the Maryknoll Sisters in bombing areas is the history of a spirit.

The attack of December 8, 1941, was not their baptism of fire. Since July 7, 1937, China had resolutely opposed the armed aggression of Japan. Cut off to a great extent from the rest of the world, lacking essential industries, with much of her richest territories under enemy control, China by her sheer refusal to recognize defeat, divided the military strength of Japanese forces.

For the Sisters, their initial experience of organized warfare—as opposed to the internecine battling of bandits versus bandits—was in Shanghai, that metropolis in the Yangtze delta. The introduction to *Shanghai Silhouettes,* the convent diary reads:

Shadows of war stalk a Shanghai enclosure. A large compound with two groups of four pavilions each, dominated and separated by a Church, was built in 1935 by the great Chinese Apostle of charity, Lo Pa Hong, and devoted to the service of China's hitherto neglected ones—the mentally afflicted. A group of German Brothers cared for the men, Maryknoll Sisters were in charge of the women. The diary entries between August, 1937, and the New Year, 1938, were made while bomb-laden planes manoeuvred above the sanitarium; refugees trudged past from out the beleaguered city and soldiers tramped in; the stricken sought sanctuary within the convent gates; food, water, and fuel dwindled, and the tallow candle sputtered its superiority because independent of electric plant and dynamo.

The status of Americans until the entrance of the United States into the war was not that of enemy aliens, but of neutrals caught between two belligerent foreign nations.

It took the war a little time to reach toward Pei Chiao, a Shanghai environ, but by August 20, 1937, aircraft extended the fighting zone beyond the Mercy hospital compound. What had first seemed another "incident," took on a serious aspect, so two of the Sisters ventured into the city for business purposes—and to size up the situation.

Shanghai is always intriguing—where it is Chinese it is deeply Oriental, where it is foreign it is overlaid with wide macadamized streets, luxurious homes, magnificent clubs, smart shops, yet both races look at ease in either section. But this time the broad avenues were banked with sand bags, fenced by barbed wire; machine guns were everywhere in evidence; caterpillar tractors were as numerous as yellow taxis around Grand Central. . . . The Bank advised us to draw out *all* our money in gold—we did—without embarrassing the institution or burdening ourselves. Furthermore, we were warned to go home quickly, as a raid was expected.

Various entries give a kaleidoscopic picture of war, not in its great sweeps but as it passes a hospital gate:

September 25. A spy was caught in the little village, five minutes walk from here. He confessed that the trench behind our place was to have been bombed last night. He was to give the location signal at nine. A plane kept the rendezvous, and hovered over the hospital for two hours. That day, the men from the hospital happened to cover the trench and it could not be located! Our cholera-typhoid injections are due. Troubles come not single spies but in battalion.

November 1st. War closes in on us—as the Chinese retreat towards Sikawei and the Japanese troops advance. We have enough rice for two weeks. A communique advises that we are in danger of being cut off from Shanghai, but what can we do?

Over four hundred insane would create quite a housing problem in the French Concession!

November 5th. Chinese soldiers from Shanghai trek past all day. Such thin little underfed boys—one wonders how they held out through three months of fighting. It is reported on good authority that Japanese troops have landed near Ming Hong. If the armies decide to fight, we may find ourselves as sandwich filling.

November 8th. From two in the afternoon on, Japanese airplanes swept the road with machine gun fire, mowing down soldiers and refugees en route from Shanghai. Some three hundred soldiers found our wall but poor protection.

November 9th. Many refugees and soldiers were admitted early this morning. Most of them had slept in the open fields last night. The wounded soldiers were brought first to the hospital where Dr. Cheung, the Brothers and the Sisters gave first aid; then they were moved into the little houses across from our compound. We hated to do this but we had promised the Consuls not to take soldiers into our place, as hospitals caring for soldiers are bombed. We carried hospital clothes and blankets out to the soldiers and made them as comfortable as possible. They were appreciative.

November 11th. Our truck went to Pei Chiao, carrying searchers for wounded men. The driver was injured and was carried back by villagers; one other man returned; no word of coolies, and the car has been taken. This is the anniversary of Armistice Day—the end of the war that was to end war!

November 12th. Today began for us about two-thirty A.M., when we thought the war had settled down in our back yard. The convent, the nurses' home, and the amahs' quarters face the firing line. We could hear distinctly the shouts of soldiers "*Sah, Sah*—Kill, Kill!"; the crying of women and children; the barking and snarling of dogs. Each time the soldiers made a charge, the bugle blared, and there followed a terrific cannonade and shouting. All the Sisters and nurses went on duty as an emergency measure.

All morning refugees poured in. We have three hundred now, in addition to four hundred insane patients.

At noon, we were notified of the arrival of the Major of the Japanese troops—bearing flowers for us—amid such suffering and carnage! He promised protection for the hospital, and granted permission for us to remove the wounded soldiers into one of the pavilions. . . . We summoned courage to ask about our truck but he said he had no truck. At that psychological moment, it rolled by loaded with soldiers of the Mikado. Without blinking, the Major asked for a loan of it for a few days. This visit is probably the prelude to daily inspection.

November 14th. Our car jolted to Shanghai. . . . The city is in a very piteous condition. Nantao, the little Chinese section off the French Concession, has been taken by the Japanese. The place is in flames and the Chinese are trying to get into the Concession. There is a small safety zone which a French priest is taking care of—it is wet and cold, and the people are hungry. Some of the better-off classes are throwing bread as it is impossible to gain entrance.

All day long Japanese troops marched by. They are so well equipped and so healthy compared to most of the Chinese we see.

Two of our boys, who have been missing several days, were returned by the Major. They had many interesting experiences. One boy is a Christian, the other a pagan. The former instructed the latter in the fundamentals of Catholic Doctrine, particularly on Baptism, sorrow for sin, and eternal life. When the pagan asked for Baptism, his companion was at a disadvantage from lack of water, but he remembered his catechism and though he did not call it Baptism of desire, he told his friend to be very sorry for all the bad things he had done, and to wish hard to see God in heaven!

November 15th. The soldiers are looting the countryside. However, some of our farmer-refugees entered here as Noah did the Ark, bringing their cows and sheep with them. The rice situation is again desperate.

November 16th. The parade continues. We wonder if all Nippon's soldiers are passing us in review.

November 17th. A truck load of boys, the cars with two Sisters, Brothers, and Miss Ling went out in search of food. But at Pei-Chiao, they fell upon sadder duties. The Brothers and boys buried forty-four bodies while the Sisters and Miss Ling searched the shacks for wounded or dead. In one place they found a lad, who with leg torn by a shell, had crawled away. He spent five days in a straw shack, wound unattended. He was put in the truck and brought back to the hospital.

November 19th. Two Sisters, a Brother, and Miss Ling went to Moa Chow. They visited the Church there, which the soldiers had ransacked. The Blessed Sacrament, the priest had saved, but the vestments were torn in shreds, the monstrance crushed, and the ciborium stolen. One of the priest's 'boys' was killed when he tried to save some articles.

The group rounded up three wounded soldiers, a cow, three sheep, and a goat—all starving. They are receiving first aid of various kinds on our compound.

A Brother took some boys out to a nearby lake and dragged out and buried about forty bodies. At the same time, some Sisters searched huts and found many more dead.

Two Sisters and Miss Ling again to Moa Chow in quest of eggs and rice. On the return trip, they looked into all the houses. These homes were owned by wealthy Chinese, who left hurriedly as the Japanese troops advanced. The soldiers billeted there and wrecked most things of value—furniture, paintings, chinaware. In the home of one of Miss Ling's friends, was found intact, a piano, an organ, and a violin. Miss Ling asked the Sisters to remove them for safe keeping and against the day the owners return. We were glad to fall heir, even temporarily, to the instruments. Our singers are not certain if their voices need tuning, or the piano.

A supply of hospital goods was hailed with delight. Our stock was low and we have cared for so many wounded.

November 24th. Three Sisters, Helpers of the Holy Souls, sought refuge with us. They went into hiding when the Japanese arrived.

This afternoon, our Sisters went out with the boys again and buried the last soldier—at least, it was the only body found. Altogether, over six hundred have been buried. We have established a large God's Acre, for we buried them in the same section as far as possible.

November 25th. Thanksgiving Day, and we have so much for which to give thanks. This is probably the only hospital on Chinese territory in this section, which has not been destroyed, and where lives have not been lost.

We observed in the American spirit—with our star-spangled banner above mantle place, and patriotic songs, sung to the salvaged piano. Our turkey, which was stew, was very good and filling.

November 27th. A boat with rice for us arrived yesterday at Ming-Hong from Sunkiang, but the pass for it had gone to Shanghai, and the head man was 'Solly' but not able to release. Today, Brother went after it again, and his persistence was rewarded. This time he brought home the bacon in the form of two hundred sacks of rice. Here, where rice is the staple food, the

Lord's Prayer is construed: "Give us this day our daily grain." Brother attributed much of his good fortune to the humor of his refugee driver. Many times he gets through places by his wit. This man is a pagan, but when he found two little flowers blooming in this shell-torn countryside, he gently gathered them, and asked us to put them on the altar.

November 28. We have been carrying our drinking water for some time from the well across the road from our building. This morning, when two Sisters went out with the boys for the water, they were dismayed to have a group of twenty Japanese cavalrymen come down to water their horses.

November 29th. This afternoon, Father Jacquenot came out with the Japanese Consul General. They are visiting all Catholic places. It was getting late, so they remained only a few minutes. No one travels after dark without urgent cause.

This Father Jacquenot is the hero priest of Shanghai. It was he who introduced in China the idea of neutral or safety zones. Its application in the early days of the Sino-Japanese war won rightly for Father the title of Protector of the Masses. Jean Wilcombe is quoted in *The China Digest,* January, 1939, as follows:

The most amazing story of all comes from a famous Safety Zone of Nantao (a city adjacent to Shanghai), where among a population of some three hundred thousand poverty stricken humans, at least one hundred thousand refugees are camping in safety. . . . Fed, doctored, kept clean, educated, helped to birth and burial after death—all within a safety zone defended by nothing more than the terrific prestige of the fearless noncombatants who founded the sanctuary, and in particular, by the prestige of a one-armed Catholic Priest who is one of the most dramatic personalities of the Humanitarian front.

December 2nd. Our three great shortages are rice (now temporarily relieved) shoes, and water. We are very careful of our little water, but today the experience of a week ago was repeated, and on a bigger, but not better, scale. About fifty Japanese cavalry men, with their horses, made inroads on our supply. Finally, we persuaded the soldiers to water their mounts at the canal. A little later, some two hundred soldiers entered the compound, and at the kitchen, filled—themselves, their canteens, their hot water bottles until our water supply was exhausted. They were not at all disorderly, nor discourteous. Some of them gave the children cookies, and one paid for his water with a box of sweet crackers and some sugar.

We went to the abandoned Ming-Hong school today and brought home some school supplies. Tomorrow, the school bell will sound on our compound. These refugee children of ours must be taught!

So, the liberty of children the world over is curtailed by school. One recalls the teacher who quoted appropriately one morning in early June: "What is so rare as a day in June," and the facetious reply—"Two days, Sir."

December 4th. Some Japanese soldiers put up in Suejaw village. They left in a hurry this morning, leaving some valuable maps behind them. When the loss was discovered, they returned to the village, and not finding the papers, rounded up some sixty Chinese men, eight of whom they shot as an example to the others. Of what? The maps were found where they had left them so the remaining prisoners were released. The father of several of our *amahs* was among the executed. A small boy who had been stabbed in the back and through the lungs was brought to us. He is a little Buddhist and hates everything Christian—ourselves included.

December 5th. We reveled in a fairly quiet day. With word that there was coal in Ming-Hong, the Brothers fared forth, and in three trips brought home quite a supply. Our lot has been made much easier by these German Brothers who have charge of the men's pavilions. They draw no lines of mine and thine—and think and act for the welfare of the entire compound.

December 10th. More soldiers on the way and many young girls are coming in for protection. To cheer up our spirits, we took out our Christmas decorations and discussed the 'what' and 'how' to do for the great feast.

December 11th. To prove that the passes to Shanghai were good, two Sisters went in. At the consulate, they picked up the money which Mother Mary Joseph had cabled and which had been held in safe keeping until we could collect. Our first investment will be in coal and—rice.

December 13th. Three priest refugees have come in this week —all disguised.

December 15th. The Hospital Staff—the Catholic members —is renewing its spirit by a retreat of three days.

Two Sisters went out in search of cotton to make blankets. Net results—some cabbages.

December 18th. Seven more bodies were buried today. One, we recognized as one of our own boys who disappeared over a month ago, when he went with a group to bury some soldiers.

December 19th. Three persons, shot by bandits, were brought in to us today. Are the gentlemen of the hills going to add to our troubles?

December 20th. A large troop of soldiers in this sector again. So no evacuation of refugees yet.

December 21st. Under cover of darkness a man stole in from Sose district by way of the fields. He brought word of the shooting of two Chinese priests who were attempting to protect some young girls—some of them native virgins from Sikawei. This morning, two of the Brothers went to the Bishop with a letter the man brought. Sose is a trouble spot—as Chinese soldiers are hiding in the surrounding hills and make sorties on the Japanese.

December 23rd. During recreation, we made and filled stockings for the refugee children. We are trying to remember everyone, though even an orange and a few pieces of candy aren't easy to manage.

We are told that during the war was a good time to study the patients' mental condition, as those with a deep psychosis would not be upset. If this be a correct test, all of ours are true mental cases. Air engagements take place above the hospital—the patients go right on eating. However, three months of this noise in addition to food shortages is telling on them. We can not make them understand why rice is not abundant.

Christmas. Gloria in excelsis. The church bells, silent these last months, rang in the feast of the Saviour. When we reached the Church the nurses, help, and refugees were in their places. The first Mass was a Solemn High, the two following Low Masses, at which the Brothers sang carols. Then we crossed to the Convent, and there we made our pilgrimage to the three cribs—as our Sisters were doing everywhere. How small the world seemed for those blessed minutes.

At ten A.M., the patients had their party in the occupational therapy room. At noon, we ran off the *amahs'* special celebration. Tea was held for the nurses at two-thirty, and at four the big social event occurred—the Christmas party for the refugee children. All those free from duty appeared—three priests, the Brothers, the officials from Pei-Chiao, the nurses, amahs and coolies. The Sisters were hither and yon, seeing to it that no one was overlooked.

One of the Brothers gave out the gifts. In lieu of a Santa Claus costume, he wore a bishop's robe—not too inappropriate, for St. Nicholas, progenitor of Santa, I believe, held hierarchical rank. The glee club, composed of the best patients—judged as to mental condition as well as vocal—sang carols. Miss Ling explained the meaning of Christmas, and wound up by calling—three cheers for the priests, three more for the Brothers, another round for the Sisters. The children made the welkin (whatever that may be) ring. Some football team might do worse for a cheer leader! All went well—and finally the guests bowed themselves out and we bowed them out until our heads bobbed automatically. Every one was happy—and we were so grateful for the gifts from our convents and our homefolk that made possible this simple keeping amongst pagans in a war-ridden land, the birthday of Christ.

A visit to the soldier patients, bearing little gifts—and then to our family gathering—a different, but our happiest of Christmases ever!

December 27th. Word over the radio that Mr. Lo, China's great patron of charity, was killed—and at the hands of his own countrymen. He lived long enough to receive the Last Sacraments and thus fortified, went to meet the God he had served so faithfully. The end did not come to him as a surprise. When he agreed to serve on a commission designed to bring some order in Shanghai and some help to his charities, Mr. Lo knew his action was open to misinterpretation. He told us then that he was a marked man. Spendthrift with his vast energies, spiritual and physical, he has been these past months. Many of his institutions wrecked, his personal fortune swept away, he calmly went his way—from hospital to camp, to refugee quarters, preaching the doctrine and baptizing those who sought it. His like is found but rarely in any land. The Bishop in tribute disclosed that Mr. Lo's every act since he was eighteen was done for the glory of God. Being human, he made mistakes, but never did he lose sight of his goal, the salvation of souls.

The year closes with over a thousand inhabitants on the compound. "And so" as Major Bowes used to say on his radio program—aeons ago, when we tramped the Westchester hills near his home, "we spin our wheel of fortune, and around, around she goes, and where she stops nobody knows"—but God.

By the time China was in the seventh month of her seventh year of strife, Maryknollers in the southern bombing area had a wide experimental knowledge of aerial warfare—extending from false alarms to direct hits. They had spent a not mean proportion of their lives in shelters or out on hillsides. Yet these occurrences were accepted by the Sisters as passing interruptions in the routine of doctrinal instruction, of home visiting and novitiate training; of care of the orphans, the blind, the old; of dispensary activities and of sodalist programs; of organization and administration of soup kitchens; of language study and teaching; of recreation and of small scale farming; of travels by train, by sampan, by bus, by chair, a-foot. Sister Imelda in a letter to Mother Mary Joseph, dated February 18, 1944, puts into writing the philosophy of life that enabled the Sisters to bear the burdens of the years—sweetly:

We have at last reached Kaying. The journey from Kweilin was long as we had delays which stretched the usual three day trip to a week.

On the first lap of the journey, we were machine gunned by enemy planes. It was the narrowest escape that some of us ever had and we have had some close calls. In spite of it all, we did thrive on the journey. *All one needs is to know how to relax and make the best of what one has at one's disposal.* Actually, I think, we gained weight on the trip—living in Chinese inns, eating delicious Chinese food, and sleeping about twelve hours each day of the seven it took to reach Hakka-land. Besides, we enjoyed everything and laughed heartily and long over many things.

Here is a detail of one of the incidents of the pleasant trip!

We were machine gunned forty kilometers outside of Kukong —in the same vicinity that we had to run on our way to Kweilin. Only this time it was more serious for the protecting bushes must have moved, too. There was no place to go for shelter. Sister Rita Marie was in a short "foot" of a hit. The buses were quite riddled, but no vital part seemed involved, as they were able to proceed under their own power.

It was early in 1939, that a bomb struck a Maryknoll mission, and flying shrapnel felled Maryknoll-in-Loting's pastor, Father Kennelly. Sister Monica Marie, a nurse, sped to his rescue armed with a competent first-aid kit. As Sister was dressing the wound, a sizable one, a second bomb landed in the compound. The concussion knocked the bottle from Sister's hand. The patient lived to report:

This was a real calamity as medicine is scarce these days. We both prayed. Heaven seemed to be our destination. Then as a heap of earth went up in the air, Sister remarked "there goes your house." I put up my hand as if to keep the debris from burying us alive. As the atmosphere cleared some, I forced a sickly smile in response to Sister's, "Never mind, the flag is still there."

When the Maryknoll Sisters' first Training School for Women Catechists was opened in Pingnam, in 1939, the city was being subjected to frequent bombing attacks. Air-raid alarms, sometimes three in a day, sent Sisters and students scurrying to the river for safety, thus interrupting the daily class routine. In order to avoid this, sampans were hired. For several weeks the student catechists spent their days on these tiny boats, on which classes were held, food prepared, and meals served. Finally, in December, 1939, when the bombing grew more severe, sixteen bombs having been dropped on the city in one hour, the school was removed to an inland village.

Sister Richard recorded that the third of March, 1940, "dawned a Monday, wash day, and rainy." The early morning alarm was so regular that it had become routine in Yeungkong. But the warden put in a personal appearance to announce the approach of uninvited guests. They came—airway and road way and water way—with much firearm work. Father Bauer's old Dobbin, ambling home with his master, took a nick or two. It was to be a busy week.

Tuesday morning, the Sisters found a door leading from the court to the street, knocked in. Then demanding military insisted on a thorough examination of the buildings. The day was made more horrible by pigs squealing a last farewell; chickens cackling a final protest; doors caving in under well planted boots; and planes diving low and soaring high, only to dive again.

The fifth was a repetition of the fourth—the Sisters circumventing the visitors by keeping the young girls out of sight. Towards evening, three of the soldiers became unmanageable, attempted to use physical force and threatened to shoot Sister Dolorosa. Good lung power brought help. The priests were reporting the case to a Japanese officer when they received word that there were two more intruders at the convent. The officer grabbed his cap, and ran down the alley to the scene. Once there, in a language foreign to the sisters, but in tones of unmistakable authority, he gave orders and the soldiers were happy to depart intact. Precautions were taken however. One door to the street was bricked up—thus discouraging entrance, and Father Bauer was installed as protector.

Marksmanship was tried out in the classrooms on the sixth day. Also inquiries were made as to local diseases. Sister Richard, R.N. waxed expansive on the subject! Bonfires raged late into the seventh night. The destruction was wanton. Goods were stolen or deliberately ruined. The streets were shambles. In a day or two the Chinese proprietors were back at their usual stands, fixing up their shops, and grateful that materials on order had not been delivered previous to the enemy visitation. There is great resilience in the Chinese.

No one knows China by knowing Hong Kong or Shanghai. She must be studied in her industrious people, leading most simple lives in the dirt courts of their bamboo-shaded homes in the thousand of tiny villages and towns that dot her great expanse.

Yeungkong in Kwangtung Province is typically Chinese and it holds a special place in the affection of Maryknollers. There was founded the first all-American Catholic mission in China. The early missioner returning there takes note of civic advancement. A newcomer from the States thinks it an authentic piece of old China. Neither is wrong. *Shop Yi Kaai,* the main street, has been widened. People may walk abreast or pass going in opposite direction—even when burdened with baskets slung on long poles and carried across the shoulders, according to the express system of the land. There is now electricity though weak of watt and low on voltage. On the other hand, Main Street is narrow according to western ideas, and *Chow Pooi Kaai* (Wine Cup Street), or *Wing Fuk Kaai* (Everlasting Happiness Street), or *Maai Po Kaai* (Buy Cloth Street), are single lanes where man and beast and chair fight for precedence. Many of the high-sounding street names are merely descriptive of the business transacted thereon. Much selling is done over out-of-door stalls. The restaurateur may have his charcoal stove on the street and serve his meat balls straight from fire to—hand. Stores may or may not have glass windows and no two buildings hew to the line. The unpredictable juttings as well as the graceful curves that mark Chinese architecture evolve from the belief that evil spirits travel in straight paths and that vagaries of line lead them astray! To the newcomer only the beautiful rounded mountains have a familiar look—the hills of home.

In 1941 Yeungkong was still in trouble, and in 1942 and on, until Easter Monday, 1944, when the Sisters in immediate advance of a new invading army, brought to safety their older girls. Earlier, twenty-five had been removed. Work could no longer be carried on. The presence of Americans was an extra hazard for the Chinese, so the Sisters joined the refugee bands traveling the roads of China.

In September of 1943, three Maryknoll Sisters and eleven school children had a narrow escape. Two out of the three Sisters in this Wuchow episode, were survivors of the Hong Kong bombardment.

The air raid siren had given a warning at five-thirty on the morning of the bombing, but that was nothing new to the inhabitants of the oft-bombed city of Wuchow. At seven fifty-five the signal sounded again, but this time it beat excitedly, sputtering forth the news that enemy planes were very near. Almost simultaneously came the dull hum of winged motors; at least forty two-motored bombers and fighter planes were flying in attack formation over the city.

The three Maryknoll Sisters were at their prayers in chapel when the second alarm came. Near the altar knelt Sister Henrietta Marie and Sister Agnes Virginia. In the rear, with eleven of the school children, was Sister Mary Chanel. Quietly Sister Chanel rose and with the children moved closer to the altar. That move saved their lives. A moment later there was a thundering din, a crash of timber and bricks; the rear of the chapel was crumbled to dust. The eleven children remained calm, riveted to their kneeling posture by the presence of the Sisters. Huge doors ten feet high tore from their hinges and smashed across the pews and benches. Stout beams crashed downward splintering themselves at the sides of the kneeling figures. Strong candle sticks on the altar were bent and twisted by the awful concussion. The very place where Sister Chanel and the children had knelt but a moment before, was now buried beneath three stories of wreckage. Not one of the fourteen people in the chapel sustained even a slight bruise.

Sister Mary Paul, visiting Wuchow in February 1944, found considerable air activity.

Unfortunately, I chose the full moon period for my visit. We spent last night from 12:15 until 5:30 A.M. on the hillside, with planes calling on us and dropping a few cards. . . . Just three nights ago, we were up from 1:30 until 4:30, and we had spent the early part of that evening from 9:00 until 10:30 on the hillside. This morning, fortunately, Father came early and said Mass immediately, so, although we all looked like wrecks, we did not have to fast too long.

The caves seem quite substantial but not as strong as the limestone ones at Kweilin. The Sisters are fortunate in being so close; it takes less than three minutes to get there.

She commended the Loting one, the most appealing feature about it being it was on the compound grounds! Sister Paul is an authority on shelters.

As the bombs dropped, the cost of living soared. Food was not rationed but curtailed by the simplest of economic systems, the "have, have not." It required deep thought and hard labor to provide anything approximating a sustenance, much less a balanced diet. "Wheat and corn ground and roasted with a bit of syrup and salt" may make a "fair substitute for coffee" but

Sister Ignatia writes to Mother Mary Joseph in praise of the real essence:

We are celebrating your birthday. This morning Father Trube sent over a cup of raw coffee to have for dinner. Real, honest to goodness coffee, and the note had in Chinese *Happy Feast,* and in English HAPPY MOTHER'S BIRTHDAY. We enjoyed the aroma, the taste, and even the last drop against which Maxwell House seems to have a grudge!

In a letter from Wuchow, dated February 29, 1944, Sister Paul touches deprivations which, though not material, cause real suffering:

One of the "most missed" things of this topsy-turvy period is word from home, letters from friends, news of the outside world. From Kweilin, the British send weekly a digest of radio bulletins with little commentary; from Chungking, there comes an American weekly sheet with a page on the happenings of the week and reprints—four or five—from magazines at home on topics of the day. That sounds pretty good, but actually many of these bulletins never find their way through the mails, and, if they do, they are, at very least, a month late. The magazine articles reprinted are very good, but they, too, are old. In one, under date of February 11, we read reprints from October 1943 *Newsweek!* When all this turmoil is over, we are going to have a feast of reading so you must remember to tell us of the worth while articles and books in the period.

We often hear the planes and sometimes see them, even if they do not stop at this popular target, but we rarely know where they went or what they did. A good training in curbing one's curiosity. We seem to have acquired the habit of just taking what comes and not being too curious about what's happening elsewhere. But, that is not voluntary. It is a necessity of present circumstances and one we'll be very glad to do without.

Madame Chiang Kai-Shek, wife of the Generalissimo, paid tribute: "The Catholic missionaries have hurled themselves unsparingly and with consecrated zeal into the task of alleviating pain and misery. . . . Their all-embracing charity is like manna dropped in the way of starved people." It was the great joy of the years that a service could be given the people so tried. Statistical procedures are of secondary importance, in the face of a national calamity. Recent figures are inaccurate and incomplete. However, some idea of the number of human beings involved in the beginnings of what has become probably the greatest hegira in history may be had from figures quoted by *The Chinese Recorder,* August 1940:

During the first year of the war the total of refugees housed and fed throughout the country (by the Catholic Mission) was 487,088. This calculation includes only those who were the guests of the various missions for a period of several months. During the second year, the number cared for was 433,819.

Before the evacuation of Kweilin, in the summer of 1944, the city population had increased from 50,000 to 400,000 during the war years. At least three different communities sought refuge there. A letter received February 1944 from Monsignor John Romaniello, M.M., Prefect Apostolic of Kweilin, tells of the united efforts of the Sisters to stem the tide of cholera which threatened the city.

The Sisters spent two weeks at the cholera hospital. Under their good care many of the patients recovered.

The missioners baptized ten or more patients a day. This might sound bad for the ministration of the Sisters, but the people are afraid of the hospital, and delayed coming. Many of the cases were too far gone for anything to be done for them. However, when word got around to the people that the Sisters were in the hospital, the patients came at an early stage and many were thus saved.

In further service to the needy, the Maryknoll Sisters established two medical dispensaries, with Sister Antonia Maria, M.D. in charge. These functioned twelve hours daily. Side by side with this corporal work of mercy, two doctrine schools were opened, one at the North Gate and one at the South Gate of the town, to take care of the increasing requests for instruction in the Faith.

Yeungkong dispensary for the year 1940 treated over forty thousand patients. Describing the dilemma of the mission nurse, in view of the shortage of supplies coupled with increasing numbers of refugees seeking aid, Sister Francis, superior at Loting, writes:

Poor folks from more disturbed areas are flocking in in great numbers. Sister Monica Marie looks at the patients and tries to find some medicine for them, when she knows in her heart that good food is what they need. Many of these poor souls come daily and it is heart breaking to give so little. Many seek spiritual aid, thank God.

The orphanage at Macao was started by two Maryknoll Sisters, who, early in 1942, were escorted, together with their Bishop—Bishop Paschang, under guard from their mission in Kongmoon to Portuguese-owned Macao. Refugees were piling into the town, and under Bishop Paschang's guidance the Sisters put their hands to the first job at hand—providing shelter and care for children. Sister Mary Paul describes the work:

In Macao, the land is flat and sun-baked with hardly a foot space for the Sisters and more than four hundred dirty, ragged, diseased street beggars filling up every square inch. When I was there, the children were coming in faster than they could make double-decker wooden bunks to accommodate them, so instead of one child lying lengthwise on a shelf, five slept crosswise. That situation has been corrected now.

There were many pathetic sights. One nice Catholic girl about twelve years old came. She saw that each one had two bowls of rice in the morning and in the evening, so one day after breakfast she waited for Sister and asked, "If I always eat only one bowl of rice, may my mother come to stay and have the second bowl?" Her mother had once been fairly well off, but was now selling some little things on the street and at times could not make enough to get her rice.

The work in Macao was not the first of its kind for these Sisters. In the five months before their departure from Kongmoon, these Sisters had fed 75,000 starving refugees. The rice line grew from two hundred a day in the first period to 2000 at the end! An earthquake, a typhoon, and the shelling of the city by a gunboat patroling the river, added to the confusion.

So far as actual attack was concerned, the Kaying prefecture was out of the range of battle. Perhaps for this reason, it was a special haven for poor creatures wandering the roads of China, homeless, helpless, often hopeless. The mission ran a Relief Kitchen—supported in part by the Red Cross, in part by donations from the few natives who "have," by little plays given by the children under the care of the Sisters, and by funds forwarded from the Maryknoll Sisters' Motherhouse. In January, 1944, Sister Magdalena estimated that they were feeding something over 20,000 monthly.

The finest thing has been the charity of the poor to each other. In visiting the makeshift shelters of the refugees the Sisters met with some striking instances of this. One woman who went daily to the mission for rice was found to be sharing this pittance with two blind women. In an abandoned one-room hut, they found a half-starved couple, the husband's aged mother, and two strangers who had sought shelter—one a leper and the other a lunatic.

Then the Japanese push that sent hundreds of thousands of refugees northwest to Kweilin was met by their victorious army sweeping south from Changsha. The enemy moved fast the summer of 1944! The Maryknoll Sisters joined the homeless throng.

Their cloak they will get from the sheen of the grass,
And a roof from a singin' word.

9

"A Lamp to My Feet"

THE oriental odysseys of the Sisters have a distinct Pauline flavor:

> In journeying often, in perils of waters, in perils of robbers, . . . in perils in the city, in perils in the wilderness, in perils in the sea.

Missioners seemed to have been spared that keenest of sorrows, the betrayal by false brethren. Sister Paul during her years of wandering called often upon her patron, the Apostle to the Gentiles.

The first great Maryknoll exodus was from Japanese-held Hong Kong to Kweilin, in the Province of Kwangsi, reached by circuitous route to Macao, and thence to Kwangchowaan, the gateway into Free China. It was somewhat of an adventure when, on January 23, 1943, armed with passes, medical certificates, and boat tickets, the Sisters boarded the *White Silver Maru*. At twelve, noon, the boat sailed out by way of West Point and through the channel that separates Lantau from the mainland. In a little more than three hours she made Macao, one of the few Asian relics of Portugal when she was a world power. Here Sister Patricia, exiled from Kongmoon, dispensed true patrician hospitality to the travelers.

It was almost a twenty-four hour trip from Macao to the bay at Kwangchowaan. The sea was smooth, and sleeping anywhere was a knack soon acquired in war lands. It was a relief to anxious minds, when the officers at the port of debarkation permitted the passengers to transfer to the small boats that would take them to shore.

But there were other problems. Sister Paul realized fully that, as welcome as they would be at any Maryknoll mission, she must plan ways and means for the Sisters to become self-supporting in works that would not cut into the diocesan activities, nor take from the fast diminishing diocesan income. Sister thought long thoughts the thirteen days it took to make Kweilin. The trip was a succession of nights at bad inns. But the Sisters made themselves at home, usually took over the hotel kitchen, and managed fair meals with the little at hand. Part of the way lay through hill country, bandit infested. It unwound like a Western movie. When two little boys armed with sawed-off guns, presented themselves as guards, the aspect was that of a comic. It was January 29th when the group reached Watlam, the first Maryknoll station on their route. The Fathers offered of their best—news, food, and a lodging in the women's quarters. Here, the Sisters had hoped for a break in the journey and a chance to rest—but for once bus arrangements could be made that assured arrival in Kweilin safe and early. On the morning of the thirty-first, after an early Mass, the group of Sisters with an escort of two Maryknoll Fathers set off for the bus station, "as gaily as tired bodies would permit," writes Sister Christella. It is she who records the hazards of the trip.

Our initial gaiety was replaced by misgivings at first sight of our vehicle. It was muddy, small, and dilapidated, seemingly incapable of carrying us, not to mention the eight hundred pounds that comprised our baggage! The driver assured us it was "seaworthy" and to have no fear. We arranged ourselves as least uncomfortably as possible about our luggage. Our quarters were cramped, but we could endure it for a few hours, if it meant breakfast in Kweilin! Meanwhile, the three busmen worked on the charcoal burner (gasoline being an exorbitant luxury), tinkered with what lay under the car's hood—it could scarcely be called an engine, glanced furtively at the tires—ashamed to look at them in the honest light—and then disappeared to have their rice. All this consumed time. It was about ten when we got started. We soon discovered that our bus had an aversion for hills and couldn't take them without help. It had rained and the road was in sad condition, but our little chariot scattered the mud with an abandon that was quite disconcerting to the rear-end chauffeurs! Our steering wheel, too, was temperamental, so we took both sides of the road without partiality. Our asthmatic horn tooted incessantly. We were in the hill country apparently, for the car stopped often. Too, it developed an unquenchable thirst, and if we weren't stalling at a hill we were stopping at a mud hole for water. At dusk we jolted into a scrubby little town, and came to a halt at a hotel which should have been brought up on charges of obtaining money under false pretenses.

February 1. Morning came at last, though it was difficult to ascertain this fact in our windowless room. We found our bus awaiting us. There were the same fruitless efforts of lighting the charcoal and tinkering with the engine. Rain began to fall, which didn't help the situation, especially when we were told we would have to walk to the river. There a pulley ferry brought us over to the foot of the hill on the other shore! By now the car was alergic even to mole hills! After we all climbed to the top, the bus decided to follow along.

Not Kweilin, but Laochow had become our objective for that day. By late afternoon everything indicated a night out in the great wide world! But by dint of hard walking we came to a town. Our previous night's experience didn't make us too eager to spend another night in a hotel, so we were a little heartened to find this one had at least a better facade. The employees, however, looked as though they had stepped from the pages of a Chinese Oliver Twist.

That night we brought our own bowls, chopsticks and spoons to the table and were most meticulous about using the hotel things—we placed a bowl of permanganate in the center of the table and we dipped everything into that before using.

February 2. The driver tinkered industriously about the car, but we weren't deceived. At a council of war it was decided that Father Downs take a bus to Laochow, with instructions that if we weren't in Laochow by noontime to send out for us. Father departed and we climbed into our own chariot and were borne along for a greater stretch than we had ever gone at one time. We were beginning to think Father Downs had made his trip in vain, when we had to get out. Climbing in and out was our day's pastime, until a mountain presented itself. The car took one look at it, ran to its foot, gasped and died completely. Disheartened, disheveled, we wearily climbed the hill, realizing the bus Father Downs would send would be our only salvation. As we dejectedly sat in a wayside tearoom trying to get a little shelter from the cold, piercing wind, a massive truck going in the opposite direction, with a Chinese soldier gesticulating from each window, attracted our attention. Thinking Father Downs was indeed on the alert, eagerly we ran to it and were helped in by the soldiers. When the volubility such an occasion always calls forth had subsided, we learned Father Downs had not sent that truck. The soldiers had seen us sitting there and they wanted to help American women. This was a government truck on its way to the town we had just vacated, and coming back it would pick up our baggage and take us to Laochow.

We decided to stick with the truck. Father Madison agreed to stay with the baggage until we came back.

We retraced the road we had taken that morning, back to the very hotel we hoped we had seen for the last time. After unsuccessfully trying to phone Father Downs not to send a truck as we had a whole army one, we went to eat. Some of the fastidiousness of the night before had been lost. Now we did not disdain to use the hotel bowls and we forgot such a thing as permanganate existed. We hurried back to the truck to find over half of it filled with charcoal. There were still two boards for us to sit on, so the soldiers tugged us in with a right good will. And for the third time that day we went over the same road, alternating between falling forward into the charcoal and the soldiers landing on top, or else falling backwards with the soldiers on the bottom.

The unkindest cut was when our little bus passed us, horn still tooting!

Laochow at last! Being with the soldiers helped us get through without presenting passports and without a baggage inspection. We were driven directly to the French mission and when we attempted to give the soldiers a *cumshaw* for their kindness, they emphatically refused it. They said they were glad to be able to do something for Americans. When we said we would tell the people in America how kind they were, that was reward enough! So here we spread the story.

At the mission, we discovered Father Downs had gone out about three o'clock with a bus for us. We ate our supper, sympathizing with him for the long ride he would have and bemoaning the fact that we would have to stay over another day. Just as we had accepted the inevitable, Father Downs appeared, so plans were hurriedly made to take the evening train to Kweilin.

Then began an epic-making walk to the station. On account of bombing, the station had been moved out of town, and as we could not get rickshaws, we walked that distance. One does not know mud until one walks to the Laochow station. We had no light, which was a blessing in disguise. I think some of us would have given up if we could have seen what we were wading through. Blindly we staggered on, our arms weary from the weight of our bags, our feet scarcely able to move from the weight of the mud. At the zero hour for our strength, the station light flickered feebly before us. Tickets were bought and we rushed in, thinking our troubles were at an end. But alas! On the train we discovered they had not the accommodations our tickets called for, so there was a delay until places could be found.

But all nights come to an end. It was the morning of the thirteenth day—and the travellers were at home in Maryknoll-in-Kweilin!

* * * *

By 1944, everyone realized that sooner or later all foreigners in South China would have to move out. The Bishops and priests were concerned about the safety of the Sisters. The Sisters were concerned about their charges. Sister Paul's policy as the danger became more acute, was to leave in a mission a skeleton staff for directive purposes so long as it could be effected with a degree of safety. This was done as Yeungkong, Loting, Pingnam, Wuchow, Laipo, in turn had to be abandoned. Each group moved on, sometimes joining a community in another town, again finding shelter in a convent from which the former occupants had only departed. The movement was always toward Kweilin. Incidents of these trips are casually recorded. From Chungking comes this narrative of the evacuation from Yeungkong:

Mass was offered at one in the morning, a hurried breakfast and we started on the road to take our girls to a place of safety before we would have to leave the interior. In the stillness about us the guns some miles to the south sounded ominously close.

The narrow path was bathed in moonlight. The shadows creeping alongside made the flight more eerie. The frightened children hardly whispered. Every one was tense—then the inevitable funny thing happened. The mission cow, part of the cavalcade, suddenly refused to budge a step further. Pulling, pushing, beating were to no avail. Sister Candida Maria, who knew a milkmaid trick or two, stepped up and gave the heifer's tail a good twist. The beast lurched away from the boy holding the rope, and went galloping off through the fields. Sister Dolorosa stayed to watch the baggage, while the rest of the party chased the cow. After the round-up, the heifer was persuaded to follow the cowboy by a mere movement in the direction of her tail.

One child lagged behind. Sister fell back with her and ever so often, Sister and girl dropped their bundles to rest. The others got out of hearing and the halting couple had to run the narrow terraces between rice fields to catch up. They hurried faster in the knowledge that brigands were famed in this section of China as robbers of fleeing refugees.

All night and the next day until noon, the Sisters plodded along with their orphans, their luggage, and their cow. They arrived ten miles out, at a tiny village where Helen, one of the former mission girls lived. Then spreading their bedding on the floor of the grain tower, the weary travelers slept for many hours before resuming their journey. All went well until Sister Candida Maria fell and sprained her ankle. It was no place to tarry, and despite the stabbing pain and swelling, the victim limped along with the aid of a stick, for another seven miles, where they found lodging for the night.

The third day, bombing was bad but the group reached Tai Pat intact—to learn that the mission they had left was badly bombed.

No method of travel offered any degree of safety much less of comfort, says Sister Dolorosa:

The Yeungkong river was higher than ever and the usual two day trip took four. The poles were too short, and at times the men helped the going by pulling on the great grasses that stretched above the floods. The lads on the shore hauled and jerked, slipped and skidded. The current was strong and against us. Living was very simple. The floor served as bed, chair, table. Our bags were our downy pillows. In the morning, we folded our sheets and our housework was done. It was hot. There was a little space at either end of the boat where we could sit and get some air, but to get in and out was all right for daintily built oriental women, not so for a strapping American woman. It required pressure to push through, on hands and knees. By the time we reached Chun Waan we were stiff and sore.

The next leg of the journey was through the mountains. The head man of the village arranged for chairs, and an escort of four soldiers. The two day trip had its risks, bandits and the danger of the bearers slipping along the narrow rice terraces. I had the good luck to sleep through much of it. Loting was fine—for three weeks, then we took to the West River toward Wuchow—and sat out an air battle that took place above us. Then on to Pingnam. We came to believe we moved there for the benefit of the American flyers. One of our missioners was acting as chaplain. Through Father, supplies came to us, which we turned into cookies and candy and sent back through the same channel. We almost missed a plane out, finishing a "last batch" for the Taan Chuk air field.

Sister Madeleine Sophie and Sister Francis trying to reach Kweilin had experiences equally as harrowing and more prolonged.

We were told to be ready by 2:30 in the morning—5:30 would bring us into the big city of Kukong. Japanese planes always started calling early and we hoped to miss them. We reached our destination, and had time to buy some northern bread and drink a cup of tea, before we heard the air alarm. Almost instantly the road began to fill up with people hurrying to the hills. They poured out of the city, mostly women and children. Infants were strapped to the back of their mothers, small ones clung to their hands, older boys and girls bore the few family possessions. All wore anxious looks, and scanned the skies frequently. We joined the fleeing crowd. A man led us to a trench in the side of the hill and we fell in flat on our faces. Everything seemed deathly still for a few moments, then we heard the ominous whir of the planes. I remember trying to pull a bush with very few leaves on it over our heads as a camouflage. Six bombs were dropped—quite close by. Sister and I said the Act of Contrition aloud. An old lady in the ditch with us wondered what it was all about and looked at us inquiringly. I pointed to the sky and joined my hands in prayer. She seemed to understand. The planes flew away only to come back in a few moments. Now they opened up their machine guns and combed the hills. What an evil sound is that rat-a-ta-tat!

When things had grown quiet, we went to the old Catholic Mission in the City—Kukong, which is also known as Shuichow—was the scene of Father Mateo Ricci's first labors in China. The Sisters convent had been leveled to the ground—the military had taken over the Bishop's house, so all we could do was cross the river to the convent on the other side. The good effects of our early morning cup of tea were wearing off after some seven hours!

It took the Sisters one month to make a trip that in ordinary times is made in ten days. There were nights spent in stations, sitting up in trains, in inns, at native homes.

On arrival in Kweilin, we piled ourselves and baggage into rickshas. Then the wheel of my wagon fell off, and my baggage slipped out with me on top. Another ricksha, and then the rain fell—in torrents! We were drenched!

In Kweilin there was no permanent resting place. Refugees and natives alike received official advice "Go West." A little group of Sisters flew in early one evening. Kwangsi's limestone mountains, rough and jagged, were outlined against the western sky. One thought of Dunsany's *Gods of the Mountains,* and listened breathlessly for the thump of stone feet. There was something fantastic about the scene! But as they pulled out that night in a box car reality pressed heavily upon them. Sister Eucharista describes the accommodations:

The train which should have left earlier in the day, was on a siding. There we found it, about ten o'clock, and soon we were stowed aboard a box car with photographic material which was being evacuated. There was a machine gun set up in the middle of the floor in case of trouble. Two American soldiers were on guard. We sat or lay on our baggage and tried to sleep. About 3:30 A.M., after much backing and shifting we started on our thirty-six hour journey. All day Sunday we broiled in the iron box car—the soldiers broke their rations with us. We fared well indeed in comparison with the poor Chinese evacuees who crowded on top the cars, in the hot sun, and even rode the cow catcher of the engine.

There were three routes out of Kweilin toward Kweiyang and comparative safety—the railroad, the highway, and the river. The first was the quickest method and the most popular, though tickets were sold at black market prices. The river route was second choice. The roads were congested with foot-weary people who had no means to pay for other forms of transportation. The exodus was swift, and remarkably complete. Just the passage of such crowds through little farms and grain fields, the starving people searching for a bit of food, ruins not alone the present crop, but lowers for years the producing power of the lands. This is an agricultural fact the world must face. The big post-war problem is not to get the people back to their homes, but to renew the face of the earth that once again it may support its people.

Sister Paul left Kweilin with the last group of Sister refugees. She relates:

The train was so crowded that in a compartment for four, thirteen and more were pressed. Aisles were jammed. There was no water, no food, no lavatory facilities. For the three days, we had to leave the train, climb every mountain, and then literally fight our way back into the train when it finally made the grade. And in China's July heat!

We are now real refugees. Heretofore, our moves were by way of our own convents. Now there is no Maryknoll wherein we may refresh souls and bodies.

Sister Jeanne Marie expresses the ardent zeal of the missioners who "dumb, silent Miltons" find it difficult to give voice to their aspirations for the future of the mission apostolate:

When with reluctance Mother Earth has shown
  Hidden against her heart her last unknown:
When in a forehead's breadth her span is brought,
  Men having found the secrets that they sought:
You still may go
Ways none yet know.

For you, in awful magnitude, abound
  Wastes, wildernesses, chasms still unfound,
Where yet undreamt of cataracts will roar
  Into unmeasured depths; and great peaks soar

Unscaled into the blue, and nameless things
  Rise from dark silent pools on flaming wings;
Where through the brush eyes cold at torrid noon
  Leap into fire beneath a nimbused moon.

To win, to master these wild virgin lands,
  There undiscovered souls your godlike hands
Will bear our Sun to be their dawn, their day;
  Then frenzied Darkness you will bring to bay:
You thus may die
Where none yet lie.

PART THREE

The North

Otto Lorenz in his [illegible] on finding Japan so definitely a [illegible] arrived there early in the year 1941. [illegible] Japan and her dependencies were very [illegible] of a tightening up and of a growing [illegible] Korea, chosen by Japan in 1910 as an [illegible] expansion, the missionaries never knew [illegible] had witnessed in 1932 the occupation of [illegible] Manchuria. For at least [illegible] Pearl Harbor attack, mission activities [illegible] severely restricted, and the detention, [illegible] called "protective" walls, in and [illegible] mission homes as if in any case [illegible] as some. But that the detection [illegible] effective but they were [illegible] and to [illegible] democratic tradition of the sanctity of [illegible] free from espionage is abhorrent. [illegible]

10

"Before the Face of His Cold"

To Father Pheur, of Fushun, Manchukuo, fell the task of carrying to His Excellency, Most Reverend Raymond A. Lane, word that a state of war existed between the home of their birth and the power that ruled in the land of their apostolate. Father had received the news over the radio. He started immediately for the center mission. As he pedaled swiftly through the busy marketplace, he saw that already it was placarded with anti-American posters!

Otto Tolischus in his *Tokyo Record* expressed his surprise on finding Japan so definitely a belligerent nation when he arrived there early in the year 1941. Maryknoll missioners in Japan and her dependencies were very conscious through the years of a tightening up and of a growing suspicion of foreigners. Korea, chosen by Japan in 1910 as an experiment in territorial expansion, the missioners never knew as a free country. They had witnessed in 1932 the occupation of Manchuria, and its re-christening Manchukuo. For at least three years, prior to the Pearl Harbor attack, mission activities were curtailed, travel severely restricted, and the detective, for other than euphonious reasons called "protector," walks in and out of their northern mission diaries as ubiquitous as any mystery sleuth—and as annoying, as some. Not that the detectives meant to be personally offensive, but they were intrusive, and to Americans, reared in the democratic tradition of the sanctity of one's home and of personal freedom, espionage is abhorrent. There was no attempt to keep this surveillance secret. Indeed, wherever Bishop O'Shea, of Heijo, Korea, went, his guard was sure to go—at the Bishop's expense!

About 8:30 on the evening of December 8, 1941, Sister Lelia and Sister Rita Clare watched some sisters as they safely crossed the compound to Fushun's native novitiate, opposite their convent.

"Sister Lelia, Sister Lelia!" Bishop Lane's voice came from the direction of the small green gate which opened from the west yard into the convent enclosure. The Sisters assumed that the Bishop with his unfailing thoughtfulness wished to assure them all was well. Shivering from the Siberian cold, without apprehension, they picked their way down the icy path with the aid of a small flash bulb. Beyond the gate, the darkness was marked by moving shades of greater darkness, the figures of many people. Snow crunched under stomping feet.

"Sister Lelia, they want us to take a look at the inside of the jail. I'll try to get back in the morning. . . . If I don't return and send you no word, you yourself are to distribute the Blessed Sacrament. My *boy* has the tabernacle keys. We don't know what is going to happen but we hope for the best. God bless you all." The Bishop's voice was clear, firm, almost casual.

Marching orders were given and all moved toward the main mission gate outside, where an army truck was drawn up. The military, about thirty—for four foreign and one native (Chinese) priest—silently surrounded the truck, and gestured the priests aboard. Father Pai, old and sick, was permitted a seat with the driver. The others swung themselves as best they could over the high body into the truck. There was no concession or courtesy that night even for the purple!

"It couldn't have happened on a better day," gaily called out Father Haggerty, mindful of Our Lady's feast, and with the nimbleness of a squirrel, he bounded into the machine. . . . The motor turned over, gears meshed, wheels whirred, then took hold. The truck moved off carefully. In the glow of its lights, we saw the Bishop with his hand raised high in blessing, as if he were commending not only St. Joseph's but every mission across the great plains, beyond the barren mountains, to the loving care of a Heavenly Father Who knew we stood in great need in this hour of peril. We waved our small torch in response—a farewell and we hoped, a signal of courage. Our feelings, though, were rather like those of small boys whistling in the dark,

confesses Sister Lelia. It was a scene enacted that night all over the Far East.

Each group of Sisters thus left behind in a mission planned and prepared in anticipation of their own arrest. They donned heavy garments, another pair of woolen stockings, perhaps a second habit. They sewed pockets in their clothes for "spares" and collected food. For Oriental prisons are not just places of confinement while awaiting trial; in themselves, they are instruments of punishment—dungeon-like and dirty, bleak and bare, cold and clammy. Nor was the idea of arrest fantastic. Before this, Sisters at various times and in different places had experienced some unpleasantness with the Japanese police.

Sister Lelia returned to Fushun from Kobe by way of Shanghai after meeting Mother Mary Joseph late in 1940. She shopped for the North, then with her companions started for *home*. At Dairen, she was arrested by the Water Police for smuggling. Sister records impersonally:

We never had, previous to this experience, any difficulty bringing materials into Dairen from Shanghai or Peking, such as we expected in transporting the same across the border—from Dairen to Manchukuo.

The Dairen Water Police, as an organization, have a very low rating in Japanese circles. The men are rude, crude, brutal. Sister Peter and Sister Lelia saw many, many evidences of these traits during their two weeks' intimate experience with them. Sister Lelia was on "parole" with the very special concession that she spend the nights at the Japanese mission. The days she spent at the police station, with Sister Peter as companion. The hours went by in endless questioning and in minute examination and re-examination of the materials involved. Every word was carefully recorded and a whole volume made of the information gleaned during the trial. This book, bound finally, was filed for further reference. So Sister Lelia is on record saying she "never committed crime before." When the courts got the case, it was dismissed on the payment of a fine of ¥600 (or about one hundred and twenty dollars gold). Before the materials, silks, cotton goods, and leather were released, two Japanese officials most politely requested "samples." They took pieces of leather, and to make it strictly a business proposition, they insisted upon paying ¥3—a nominal sum in ordinary times.

Sister Lelia was to look again on the face of pagan *in*justice. Shortly before the Sisters were removed from Fushun to Mukden, while the Japanese were trying to persuade them to *ask for* repatriation, Sister Lelia received a summons to the police station. With a companion, she answered the call. The two Sisters were brought into a room and left standing. Toward one corner were gathered many officials, crowding about something lying on the floor. The screams and cries for aid identified the something as a Chinese. With utmost cruelty and wicked glee, the men, as they circled the prostrate form, took turns beating, kicking, and pricking him. The Sisters were helpless to protest the outrage or to protect the victim. Completely shaken, the two slipped out of the room. No attention was given their departure. They never knew if they were brought in on the scene to receive an object lesson! Only face to face with old paganism, does one realize that the new pagans of the Western world enjoy the Christian dispensation of Charity!

Two years earlier, in 1939, Sister Rita Clare, on a catechetical trip to P'so Ma Ch'ang in Manchukuo with a native aspirant, was arrested by a zealous official. She was led from police station to police station. Finally, she encountered an official who ruled that so long as she was only teaching the doctrine of the Church she was innocent of any offense and he ordered her released. This judgment indirectly aimed at nursing activities of the Sisters. An aftermath of this affair was a highly amusing one: a frightened catechumen who witnessed the arrest of Sister Rita Clare rushed to the Mission and at the gate breathlessly reported to the old catechist, "Sister Kang has been taken and will be hit to death." To which Mr. Wu with characteristic Chinese imperturbability replied, "That is not important; when that Sister came here, she came with the intention of being martyred." However, the activities of the nurses were curtailed. Catechetical work continued and any appearance of being intimidated by the occurrence was carefully avoided.

At the Chinese Mission, in Dairen, the Sisters had suffered in themselves and more in their people, from the harshness of the police. Sister de Lellis, R.N., was making calls upon the sick when a policeman demanded her bag, took it to the station, and Sister was brought up on charges of treating the sick without authorization and of having in her kit a hypodermic needle—this latter was made to appear a heinous offense. It required some management to quell the anger in the official breast, and to quash the charges against Sister. There were however retaliations made on the innocent Chinese, whose ills Sister had attempted to assuage.

By evening of the first day of war, in all of Maryknoll's northern territory, only the Sisters in Chinnampo, Korea, were unprepared to set up light-housekeeping in a jail. There, a sung Mass in honor of the feast of the Immaculate Conception had been carefully and lovingly practiced by the local choir. The day came—and a single Christian was present.

Later, as Sister Elenita and Sister Gregoria discussed the non-appearance of their Japanese congregation, three detectives called at the convent and minutely interrogated Sister Elenita, an excellent language student, as to her proficiency in Japanese, her ability to read Japanese newspapers, to understand radio broadcasts, her knowledge of political affairs. No reasons were offered for the examination, but it was not difficult to believe that a crisis of some kind was at hand. Americans had been *suffered* not too kindly for a long period. It was about four-thirty that afternoon when, as the convent door was opened in response to an impatient knock, two of the morning callers pushed their way in, despite the efforts of Father Hunt's *boy* to announce them. They summoned the two Sisters to the police station. As they went to get ready, the men stalked after them into their dormitory. Wraps, passports, breviaries, the little money in the house—and the Sisters were rushed out without opportunity even to lock the door. Sister Gregoria was to discover that the open door policy made access easier for the police who searched the place in her absence. On the way to the police station, Sister Elenita managed to give part of the money to Sister Gregoria "In case—"

Dusk falls early in a Korean winter. The street lights were not on. Chinnampo has electricity, but its use is restricted to night hours. The stalls—food, shoes, clothing, that line the streets were boarded up. The few people abroad looked peculiarly square and short in the evening glow, for the weather had reached a low that called for at least two padded coats—if one possessed such material wealth. The little party from the convent trudged through the deep snow in procession formation: a small guard, two tall, slim Sisters, another small guard—the men well-armed.

Chinnampo ranks as a fair sized city, but it has few sidewalks. Despite the annual snowfall there is no effort to clear paths. A narrow passage is made in the drifts by the tread of the passersby. The police station was within walking distance. The Sisters were led into a dimly lighted office occupied by some half dozen Japanese officials, and filled to saturation with the dense smoke from the heating stove and from cigarettes. Going in from the clear, crisp cold, the two newcomers coughed and choked but were completely ignored by the men. No chairs were forthcoming so, standing in the center of the room, they proceeded to anticipate Matins. They were in the second nocturn of the Divine Office, when a guard motioned Sister Elenita to follow him. Sister Gregoria was taken to another room, unlighted, and left there for over an hour. Then without explanation of her companion's whereabouts, and with the not altogether comforting assurance that "we are Japanese so we do not mistreat people—there is no cause for worry"—Sister Gregoria was assigned the escort of a soldier and sent home.

The next day brought confirmation of Sister Gregoria's fears that Sister Elenita was in jail, and that Father Hunt, Maryknoll's pastor in Chinnampo was likewise held. The two weeks of Sister's prison sojourn were spent by Sister Gregoria in work, worry, and pedagogical pursuits. The church, the rectory, the convent had to be put in order; packing done, food prepared for the prison, which was sometimes accepted and other times rejected, and it was to be discovered later that very little ever reached Father Hunt or Sister Elenita. The helper, Anna, was faithful. The Christians were intimidated. Communication with any other mission was cut off. The police were watchful and very thorough in their search. One budding official pierced the ceiling with his sword and thrust in a hand, which he withdrew trailing cobwebs. A wire was tracked two rooms and a hall beyond only to find the end dangling loose! One day, Sister Gregoria was escorted by her personal body guard, Mr. Watanabe, to the railroad station under orders to entrain for Heijo. She toiled through the snow against blasting winds from the bay with cases and packages for herself, for Sister Elenita, and for Father Hunt, for she hoped they might be released and exiled with her. She waited and shivered—the escort, very alert, flashed his eyes hither and yon "as if watching for a surprise attack by MacArthur any moment." Finally, from police headquarters came word to return to the convent—so Sister Gregoria with bags and bundles, accompanied by Mr. Watanabe who pedaled a wheel beside her, returned. By the time they reached their destination, the two were haltingly discussing the Trappists in Japan! Nor did the police neglect to profit by what they evidently considered an excellent opportunity to learn English. Despite Sister Gregoria's protests, the teaching role was thrust upon her. On the sound pedagogical principle of proceeding from the known to the unknown, Sister took up the one subject she knew in both English and Japanese—Religion. Her methods were not unmodern. As visual aid, she used the *Jesus and I* chart! For phonics and reading she used the accompanying texts; for memory training—the Our Father, the Hail Mary, the Act of Contrition! The high spots of the time of waiting were the occasions when food was accepted at the prison; the day when the Korean aspirant sent by Sister Eugenia, Regional Superior of the Sisters in Korea, got through, and when Father Hunt from prison directed Sister Gregoria to consume the Sacred Hosts.

When Sister Elenita was led from the police office, she was

taken down to the jail cells. En route, she met Father Hunt likewise in custody. The cell block opened on a corridor where there was a desk of authority and some dozen police in attendance. No charge was made, but Sister was subjected to insult and indignities. Sister Elenita recounts her experiences to Mother Mary Joseph:

I was stripped of everything but my underwear and the tunic of my habit. They made certain I was not concealing papers. In my embarrassment, I turned around, only to find two cells full of men, pressed against the bars watching me. Most of these prisoners were decent, but a few called out coarse remarks. At that moment, I determined I would be stupid to any form of Japanese address except that of courtesy. Mother, you advised that we Sisters let our bobbed hair grow long in case we should have to adopt lay dress. Fortunately for me, my hair was shoulder length. The Japanese women traditionally wear long hair. The only exception may be a few in the international set. I think short hair would have lowered me, if possible, in the eyes of the police—although being without comb, brush, pins, or string to use as a ribbon, I must soon have appeared as a wild woman.

After the examination, the opened cell door seemed almost an avenue of escape. I was to find it had its own trials. I was never charged with a crime, I was never tried, I was never condemned to punishment, I was just forcibly pushed into a cell and locked up. I was the fifth woman in the cell. My companions were Koreans. In my fifteen days there, without the bond of a common tongue, I was to experience friendliness and kindliness, the generosity and something of delicacy of these people. I never knew of what they were accused. But when I was dismissed, as unexpectedly as I had been arrested, I had one regret—I could not return to my companions and smile my thanks.

About eight thirty o'clock on the first night, a guard called in asking if I had eaten. I hadn't since noon. In a little while he stuck through a hole in the bottom of the cell door some bread and a cup of water in a dirty tin. Twenty-four hours later another piece of bread and a tin of water were given me. Then I was put on regular service, three meals a day of poor quality rice and a red bean, as relish, a small dried salted fish or a piece of pickled turnip. One of the poor dears used to save me something from her plate, apparently thinking I needed or was accustomed to more. The little act probably called for heroic charity on both sides—she was hungry and used to but the bare essentials of life —and you know those necessities to an Oriental are pitifully scant. As for me, I regretted that I had anticipated the peck we used to say we had to take before we die! Our drink was water, a couple of cups stuck in and passed from one to another! When we returned them, they were just stacked up without washing, ready for the next time!

The toilet arrangement was a trap in the floor, uncovered, never cleaned and without privacy. We had no means of washing. It was an offense to go to sleep before ten. At that time, the guard made the rounds and would crack, with a bamboo pole stuck through the bars, any offender. I was guilty twice—the first time the roar of the guard startled me so, I hopped away from the stick; the second time one of my little friends wakened me. We slept and ate and had our living on the stone floor, below ground level, without the aid of chair, or table, or pallet, and in stocking feet and with scant clothing. It was bitter chill and cold.

These privations seemed mere inconveniences in comparison with the dreaded examinations and the daily questioning. Each morning, I with the other prisoners, was examined to see if I had acquired anything new. Each afternoon I was taken into the hall before the police. I dreaded these interviews for the men quite freely discussed me, cast doubts on my way of life, made fun of religious practices, like mocking the Sign of the Cross. I used to hope that the dirt on my face would hide the color that their obscene remarks brought to my cheeks. I stuck to my resolution of not understanding low forms of Japanese, and of observing the best form of Japanese etiquette myself.

Poor Father Hunt wasn't faring much better than I. As I passed his cell each day to be questioned, he gave me his blessing. Occasionally, when the guards were not looking, by standing close to the wall separating our cells, at the front, we could speak to each other. His voice was a bit shy, the day he asked if I'd mind if his *boy* passed me a suit of his heavies. How grateful I was! Once I had received permission from a guard to have his *boy* bring me a pair of bedroom slippers. These were almost a necessity, as the corridor floor was often sloppy wet and my feet had swollen from chilblains. I regretted this move for the next time I appeared and a guard saw the slippers on my feet, he grabbed them off, kicked them across the hall, and pushed me forcibly back to the cell. The fellow who had granted the request for slippers looked on indifferently.

This was the one and only time I cried—but the guards didn't know it. I was determined to prove to them that American women were sturdy. They consider us soft. I used my high Japanese manners with but one exception. We had a couple of dirty, torn blankets to sleep on. One day one of my companions picked up a patch that was torn off and sat on it in a corner. A guard discovered it. He accused the poor soul of tearing the blanket and went to beat her. I could not take it, and I turned in fury on him. My breath froze in the frigid air, but for once, I felt good and warm. I'm sure it must have been my looks that made him desist. I'm not small for an American, so I loom large among Orientals. And my unkempt hair stuck out at all angles! Perhaps I would have been less brave had the guard picked on someone other than my special friend. So far as I could make out from sign language this woman was the mother of a large family. Her big heart took me in and she would do little things for me, like rubbing my stiff fingers between her own worn hands.

One day a Japanese woman was put in our cell. I had not thought there was anything there to appropriate, but she did, even my very person. The rags of blankets she took to herself and then informed me I'd be her hot water bottle. So she rolled against me to keep warm.

While the hardness of the floor would not interfere with the rest of the Koreans, the lack of heat would disturb them. An adobe house has a raised platform, lined with bricks like an oven. At one end of the dais is built a stove, in which wood and dried leaves are burned; the heat from the stove goes into the flues, the smoke finds its way out by a chimney running up the opposite wall. On this *kang* the people lie down to sleep and sit up to eat. So the poorest have some degree of heat to temper the long winter of sub-zero cold. Sister Elenita continues:

Mother, I had my breviary. It is still a wonder why I was allowed to keep my book, for the Japanese seemed to suspect print not in characters. I made my horarium around the Hours of the Divine Office and it was wonderful to know that I could live the life of our Sisters everywhere. I had to anticipate Matins and Lauds, as our only light was from the corridor. The kind little women respected my prayer time and would not eat until I said Grace. After all, our "trays" didn't impel a rush to dinner, but if I delayed, one of the women would poke me and try to make the Sign of the Cross to remind me!

At first, I knew what fear was—but that gave way to a deep abiding joyousness of spirit. The beautiful Office of Saint Lucy reminded me of the Source of all strength. "When you shall stand before kings and governors, take no thought how or what to speak; for it shall be given to you in that hour what to speak; for it is not you that speak but the Holy Ghost." I shall always have particular devotion to this Office. Thereafter I faced my inquisitors with greater assurance. Then the union, the communion of Maryknoll Sisters reached into my cell. I recalled that at home in our lovely Motherhouse chapel vigils were kept day and night, and I thrilled at the remembrance of our precious Cloistered Sisters sacrificing for missioners—among whom I was privileged to be numbered. You seemed, Mother, to have enfolded us in a warm mantle of prayer.

It was long ago and far away that the inspired Psalmist sang: "He shall send out His word and shall melt them. His wind shall blow and the waters shall run."

My breviary was a good calendar. My Christmas observance I planned in advance. I would rise and keep watch from eleven to twelve on the Eve, as I knew all Maryknoll Sisters would be doing no matter what the difficulties. I had in my breviary, Mother, a Nativity card you gave me years ago. This would be the poor Crib at which I would adore the new born Babe, where I would pray my thanks for you, make intercession for the Church, the world, my native land, missioners, Maryknollers, and my poor Japanese people.

I don't think I was unduly tense, certainly not emotional. I looked forward to being held indefinitely. God was just merciful to me when everything else was taken.

So—one looks out through prison gratings to the stars!

But on the twenty-third, when I was called for the routine examination, I was told I was to be escorted home, was to pack, and leave the next day for Yeng You, where the other Sisters were being interned. At one time I had been told that Sister Gregoria was here. My clothes were returned, bearing all the marks of careful search and then being thrown down carelessly. I made the required *Thank you for hospitality toward my unworthy self* and walked out—not exactly free, but freed from jail. Soon, too, was I free from the accumulated grime of over two weeks, and I sat down to enjoy the fatted calf, produced from a tin by Sister Gregoria. We talked all night for I had to hear of Sister's experiences and to tell her my story. But we were on time at the police station, and for our train—not before a bill had been presented Sister Gregoria for my board in the jail!

It was the day before Christmas!

11

Orient Ode

SISTER LELIA always so sweetly certain in her movements stood strangely hesitant at the window of our East room, watching the rising sun turn from amethyst to rose, to pale gold. Her fair face was flushed. Between her brows was a slight crease denoting loving concern. She had spoken of the night before when she had seen Bishop Lane and his priests taken from the mission compound to the Fushun jail. Then her thoughts seemed to go back across the world to her college days at Mount Saint Vincent's-on-the-Hudson, where Sister had graduated in 1932 an English major. She quoted softly:

> Lo, in the sanctuaried East,
> Day, a dedicated priest
> In all his robes pontifical exprest,
> Lifteth slowly, lifteth sweetly,
> From out its Orient tabernacle drawn,
> Yon orbèd sacrament confest
> Which sprinkles benediction through the dawn;—*

It is Sister Celine Marie who tells this story of the morning of December 9, 1941.

Slowly Sister Lelia picked up her wrap. Slowly she walked over to the West yard, to the Bishop's chapel. With her black woolen shawl for humeral veil, she reverently carried the ciborium to the parish church where a wondering congregation was waiting. There to all who approached the rail Sister distributed Holy Communion. The good old faithful women wept quietly. Significant and characteristic of a Chinese congregation—not one

* Francis Thompson: "Orient Ode," *Poems of Francis Thompson,* Oxford.

man came up. Fervent and reverent—they were nevertheless not prepared for this feminine usurpation of man's wonderful privilege. Sister reserved enough Hosts for those in the novitiate chapel. There she communicated the Sisters, the eighteen novices and postulants, Sister Maria, who had served throughout, a gray clad acolyte, and then herself.

In the North, in Manchukuo and Korea, where the priests were arrested without warning, the privilege of caring for the Blessed Sacrament was delegated to the Sisters.

Sister Dominic at the Hopei Compound across the river distributed Holy Communion in the Church, then down at the native seminary, and later to her community and the native aspirants. "I never saw the people more reverent . . . The tears were streaming down their faces," she writes.

Police action was less precipitous but not less drastic than at Fushun, when war engulfed Dairen. This port city long had shown ever increasing signs of strain. As early as June 1941, Sister Fabiola was refused with marked discourtesy a visa to go from Dairen to Fushun. Geographically, Dairen is in Manchuria; politically, the metropolis is at the crossroads of the Far East and was considered an integral part of the Japanese Empire proper. The Kwangtung Leased Territory, of which Dairen is the pearl of price, has been a pawn in the battles of Asia. The Russians demanded this territory from China as part of the Boxer Indemnity; in their turn, Japan demanded it as a spoil of the Russo-Japanese War. For a foreigner to leave Dairen, he must have a permit from the Dairen police, and in order to enter Manchukuo, he must secure a visa from the Manchukuoan Consul.

It was on December 12th that the Maryknoll Fathers, Sisters and a Brother in Dairen were interned at *Fushimi Dai,* the Japanese mission and central house of the Sisters. In their enforced hasty departure from the Sacred Heart compound, there was no opportunity for the priests to distribute the Hosts. Father Lenahan reverently carried the Blessed Sacrament in his overcoat pocket, as he with his companions were led through lanes formed by their Chinese people, taken by tram across a city intent on its own concerns, to *Fushimi Dai* and concentration. Sister Peter describes the scene of internment:

Outside, the sky was dark, a heavy snowfall was tossing about in a wind of gale proportions. Within, we fifteen American Maryknollers were surrounded by more than twenty guards—uniformed police armed with swords and revolvers, plain clothes men, and representatives of the Foreign Office.

Through the triple barriers of darkness, paganism, and war, penetrated the words of the shepherd of Christendom: "We have been asked by the Vatican to be kind to you missionaries of enemy nations." It was the authentic voice of the Vicar of Christ, though the message was uttered in a far Eastern tongue, by a prison guard.

And in a pocket of a shabby overcoat hanging on the back of the door, was the Sacramental Christ. "Who hath gods so nigh them, as our God is present to all our petitions?"

When the Sisters at the Maryknoll Academy, Dairen were interned, Sister Sabina, Japanese, was left as guard of honor for the Lord of Hosts until a native priest was assigned.

Once, after the Americans were taken to Shanghai, Sister Sabina was privileged to bear the Blessed Sacrament from the Academy Chapel to the Church. Poverty-stricken as the little group of nationals was, for this occasion, Sister hired a *machê,* a Russian carriage, as more worthy of a Royal Progress, and accompanied by Sister Marie Elise, one time tennis champion of Manila, she carried the King of Kings through the wayward lanes of Dairen. This submissive Christ borne by men—yea, by women—must be for a lesson to a world struggling for power and domination. With the missioners interned Mass and Holy Communion became a rare privilege for Sisters Sabina, Marie Elise, and Talitha. On one occasion, however, Our Lord went to them, in a most striking manner, as Sister Luke relates:

The three Sisters were not permitted to attend Mass with the internees. One Feast Day, with fine courage, they came to the Church, but were put out. We heard the shuffling of feet and surmised what was happening. However, the Church doors were open, and the three knelt on the cold steps. I think I will never forget the burst of joy I felt, when, after communicating us, Father Lenahan (God bless him) calmly opened the gates of the altar rail, and walked down the center aisle, through the door and gave Communion to the three Sisters, Mrs. Furuya and her little girl. This under the eyes of two armed guards. But they never made a move! Tears of gratitude fell as Father returned to the Altar unmolested.

The internees in Dairen were able to arrange with the guards for two hours to be spent in church daily—one hour before breakfast which allowed for meditation and Mass, and an hour in the late afternoon, when the night office of Compline was sung and Benediction given. Single file and under guard back and forth across the frozen garden the little procession went. One of the men on duty was curious as to why the cold church had such attraction. The Catholic belief that Christ, true God and true Man, is really present in the Host after Its consecration in the Mass was explained. Thereafter, this pagan, whenever it was his task to go to the church with the internees, in deference to their beliefs, removed his cap to which was attached the insignia of his authority, stood at attention before the altar and presented his sword, then turned and watched his charges file into the pews. When the period was up, again he came to attention and presented his sword, before he signalled the worshipers to leave the place. Belloc's verse often came to mind: "It seems to me that the grace of God is in courtesy."

In Korea, at Heijo, Sister Loyola received word from Father Steinbach to consume the Sacred Species. Father in his cell heard talk that the Sisters would be arrested and he managed to send a message to the Japanese compound. In Yeng You the convent has a chapel. This is an exception rather than the rule in the missions. Usually all the buildings housing the works of a section are grouped about the church as a center. To the church, the Sisters go for their religious exercises. While this arrangement denies them a good degree of privacy and the privilege of the Blessed Sacrament reserved under their roof, it does on the other hand give the people the object lesson of daily church attendance, and a realization that religion is an intimate affair of every day living rather than a mere Sunday observance. Sister Gabriella was superior at Yeng You. Father Coxen, the pastor, had instructed her to distribute Holy Communion to the Sisters until the Consecrated Particles were consumed. A Korean priest was permitted to visit the convent under guard. He advised that a Host be reserved, so that the Sisters might have the consolation of the Real Presence. A native priest would be permitted to take over shortly. So it was that, when the Japanese authorities providentially selected the Yeng You convent as the place of internment for the Sisters in Korea, they named the only convent where the Blessed Sacrament was reserved. The Sisters reached the place on Christmas Eve and, though Christmas Mass was not possible, they had the privilege of adoring the new-born King, cradled there on the altar. Of this Sister Eugenia writes:

We did not have Mass Christmas, but it was consoling to have the Blessed Sacrament in the house. We made our visits to the three Cribs, and the attic disgorged decorations and gifts. We had great cause for joy that most of us were together again and that all were safe after dangerous days. We wondered prayerfully about our Sisters elsewhere, their well-being—for our first—and the last—radio report we had on the beginnings of the war, was of bombings over Pearl Harbor, Baguio, Manila, Hong Kong, Kowloon. It sounded as if all Maryknoll missions were under fire.

At Shingishu, the Maryknoll dispensary was watched, its activities slowed up but it was not closed. Sister Rose of Lima, one of the staff of three Sisters stationed there, describes this first war-time Christmas:

Midnight Mass was out of the question as the authorities had prohibited large gatherings of any kind. However, we were given permission for early morning Masses, but were questioned as to the number we expected would be present. . . . Christmas dawned with all the possible splendor of war-torn days. With a mingling of sad and glad feelings impossible to express, we knelt in silent adoration. "O Babe help us all everywhere with the graces we need most to meet the incidents of this day." It was not so much resignation, as willing God's Will. He alone knew the reason for it all.

So the day was brim full: three Masses, all crowded beyond the doors, Baptisms, two marriages, the return of long lapsed souls, kept Father busy until two in the afternoon. As we knelt for our daily Holy Hour at five, we were all but overcome with the Peace of the Christ Child—and gratitude to Him. But there was heartache, too, in the knowledge that close by ten Maryknoll Fathers were imprisoned and suffering from much the same privations that marked the very first Christmas, two thousand years ago.

The Ducks of Dairen deserve to take their place among the most renowned of fowl—Chanticleer, the Snow Goose of Dunkirk, the Cratchit's Christmas turkey. Sister Stella Marie tells the story:

A few months before the war our helper, Lao Chi, invested in some live ducks, and sought our permission to pasture them in our back yard. We had no objections. Every evening, Lao Chi would say hopefully, "Maybe egg come tomorrow." We always nodded an affirmative. Hope deferred never lessened her devotion to the creatures. She doted on her dear ducks. After our internment, she got in to see us, on what ingenious protest we never fathomed. When she told us she would "cut" her ducks for us for Christmas, we fully appreciated the magnitude of her offering.

We were looking out of the window on the afternoon of Christmas eve, and so saw Lao Chi waddling along the street heavily laden. As she came below us we could look down into her basket. She had put fluted paper on their legs, as she had seen us do on other Christmases, and wrapped the birds carefully in precious and rare cellophane! Courteously, she asked the guard for permission to leave the things for us. He refused, curtly. Slowly, poor Lao Chi trudged out of the gate, still holding the basket. When she reached the road, we saw her put down the bundle, cover her face with her hands, and weep. We too wept—not for ourselves, nor the loss of the ducks, but for faithful, generous Lao Chi.

A sacrifice, to be complete, must be consumed. The ducks had cost Lao Chi too dearly to allow a mere policeman, and he a foreigner at that, to deprive her of her merit or her joy. She got in contact with the Fathers' boy, Lao Wang. Next morning, about six, Lao Wang might have been seen slipping a basket into a bush before he appeared at the front door. To him, the recumbent guard presented a picture of sleeping beauty. The lad softly retraced his steps, retrieved his precious burden, padded back and entered the convent. Our kitchen brought forth a worthy festal dinner.

In Dairen, as elsewhere, the Christians had not been able to attend Mass or receive the Sacraments since the foreign priests were interned. Father Ryan made protest, and won the concession that on Christmas the faithful might attend his Mass. Confessions were allowed—at the altar rail was the stipulation, and any who wanted to go had to declare his intention at the City Hall. The internees were not permitted contact with the people, and were led in and out of the Church single file, under the eye of the law. The real trials of confinement, all missioners agree, were not primarily want of privacy, scant meals, lack of funds, but the shackling of feet that had tread the byways on errands of mercy, the strange experience of being in and not of the city, the understanding of the spiritual needs of a young Christianity and the inability to minister to them. The scriptural phrase Father Founder made so familiar to the older generation became a prayer of supplication—"No matter if Paul or Apollo or Maryknollers planted and watered, please God, give Thou the increase."

Bishop Lane and the priests of his household were released from prison after a few days, and interned, temporarily, in the Fushun rectory. Sister Lelia describes the participation of the Sisters' Christmas observance:

'Twas the night before Christmas and all through the house—not a light was shining across the darkness from the Sisters' convent in Fushun to the dimly lit rectory two hundred yards away, where Bishop Lane and the captive Fathers could be seen making preparations to celebrate the story ever old yet always new.

As "enemy aliens" the Maryknollers passing the days under strict military guard at the Fushun rectory, could not communicate directly with the Sisters. The *bamboo wireless,* however, proved its efficiency. One of the house boys calling for altar linens at the convent conveyed to the Sisters the information that, although there could be no midnight Mass in the Church, they might WATCH from darkened windows, the Bishop's three Masses, to be said in the rectory dining-room which faced the convent.

Five minutes to twelve found all the Sisters at their stations on the west side of the house and there, kneeling on the wide window sills, through double windows keeping out Manchurian blasts, they "saw" the new-born Babe raised aloft three times. With the physical barrier of two sets of double windows between them and the Midnight Sacrifice, the Sisters realized they had not actually assisted at Mass. But they had done all they could. Christ had come again to sweeten captivity, to strengthen and spur on those who in His Name were trying to spread the light of faith in the darkness of a pagan world. Uncertainty there was aplenty, but no fear, no uneasiness.

It was Christmas in Manchu-land and Christmas in the hearts of the sons and daughters of Maryknoll; for it was once more the birthday of the Little Prince of Peace Whom love had made them follow and Whom they had seen in the

> Little round white World
> Circle without end,
> Finger-poised in a human hand
> Where time and Eternity blend.

So, despite war, imprisonment, internment, danger—the holy feast of the Prince of Peace was observed triumphantly in Maryknoll's vast mission theatre—albeit the white Christmas of the North was a study in contrast to the turbulence in the South. Father Feeney in Kowloontong, had hoped that hostilities might be suspended for Christmas Day, but modern scientific warfare has no time for the lovely old tradition.

> Some say that ever 'gainst that season comed
> Wherein our Saviour's birth is celebrated,
> The bird of dawning singeth all night long;
> And then they say, no spirit dare stir abroad,
> The nights are wholesome, then no planets strike,
> No fairy takes, nor witch hath power to charm,
> So hallowed and so gracious is the time.

For seven years *birds* had come to mean one thing—enemy planes!

However, presence at midnight Mass was the privilege of the Sisters. While the concrete walls of Maryknoll Convent School shook from the terrific strafing inflicted by the British upon the victorious Japanese now entrenched in Kowloon, Mass was celebrated by Father Feeney in the Sisters' basement shelter. A high teakwood table served as altar; a metal filing case as tabernacle. No music was attempted, everything being done as quietly as possible so as not to attract the attention of the Japanese soldiery who occupied the rest of the building. The shelter wore its streamers of green and red bravely. Sister Joseph Marie achieved fudge with "substitutes" and on a brazier. The hazard from bomb and shell was too great to attempt to reach the kitchen. Boxes from the Motherhouse sent for Easter and arriving belatedly just before the blitz, provided Christmas gifts.

Sister Amata made note in the hospital in Hong Kong:

Christmas Day dawned bright and clear and everyone tried to be cheerful. Food was so scarce, work was so heavy, nerves were all on edge. All night long we had heard the rumble of guns from the other side of the mountain. Oil dumps were burning, the great drums being hurled hundreds of feet into the air after each explosion, filling the sky with great sheets of flame from which bellowed clouds of black smoke.

God had made Hong Kong so beautiful. Oh, the sorrow to see it marred by man's fury! Still there was peace in our hearts, and in the dawning there was renewed the miracle of God's Love—in the Sacrifice of the Mass. I suppose we risked our lives when we went out to scrounge gifts for the patients—but that realization is just coming upon me, now that the British Lion lies vanquished.

In only one of the six Maryknoll convents in Hawaii was it possible to have Mass at midnight in 1941, because of strict blackout regulations. On the Island of Maui, seventy miles from Honolulu, the Sisters conduct a school and home for children. The ingenious boys saw to it that the "Inn" was sufficiently darkened without to satisfy the military, and bright enough within for the celebration of Mass. The Sisters' diary records the unforgettable event:

On the 24th, the Home boys spent all day covering our very high chapel windows with blackout paper. Meanwhile, waxing, polishing and decorating went on apace inside. The evening hours flew by until five minutes to twelve. The doors were closed, the windows shut down, and one by one the large candles on the altar were lighted, revealing the huge poinsettias that flanked the altar. It was such a beautiful picture that we hated to spoil it with the harshness of electric lights. Then Father stepped out onto the altar and the Holy Sacrifice moved toward that Climax for which we had so long waited. For us Christ was truly born again and we had the grace to realize it. Perhaps it was the setting of preceding events, but our Christmas Mass was one never to be forgotten.

And at the heart of Maryknoll, just before Midnight Mass, Mother muted her grief and voiced her faith as she spoke to the Community assembled:

Where our Sisters are, or how they fare, we do not know. Whether they are cold or hungry, whether imprisoned or under fire, we do not know. One thing we do know. Wherever they are, however they fare, they are praying for us, as we are for them. Thus while our hearts are saddened, Christmas triumphs more truly than ever this year. Distance, disaster, death, nothing can break the bond that unites us all in the Heart of our Infant King, in Whose tiny omnipotent Hands we lovingly entrust our Sisters today and every day.

12

Changing of the Guard

THERE comes a time, in every protracted trial, when it resolves itself to a question of endurance. To the internees in the North, the constant shifting of the guards was a perennial cause of apprehension. Potentially, each new one was an enemy, until he could be classified. By the two hundredth, the Dairen Maryknollers found that they fell pretty well into categories. All were respectful, some were gruff and unbending, others were kindly disposed, most were indifferent. To the Chinese and Koreans, the guard duty meant usually little more than a day's work with a miserable pittance attached upon which they and their families existed. The imperial policy, as witnessed in these annexed lands, was to save for the loyal Japanese all positions of honor and all good salaried jobs.

The guards worked in shifts, so a group was always on hand and operative. They not only watched while the internees slept, ate with them, took them to church, supervised their work, but they planned their schedule! If it were something unusual for Japanese police to make out an horarium for religious, they went at it with assurance. Hours for rising and retiring, for meals and community prayers were set. "A second novitiate according to the *cop*-tic rite," remarked Sister Luke. Occasionally it was somewhat of a shock to have a meditation terminated by a gruff voice declaring, "time up" in place of the customary "Resolution." The number of guards always available might indicate either plenty of man power, or an over evaluation of a missioner's political importance. The truth probably was a lack of a concerted plan in regard to religious. For as guard changed unto guard, so internment admitted of various moves, and the few exceptions to the rule of concentration were without reason. If this variability counteracted the monotony, it added to the sense of insecurity.

In Dairen, the set-up for the Maryknollers was peculiar in itself, and lasted until February, 1943, when the group was taken to Shanghai. In a convent designed to house comfortably not more than four women, in reckless disregard of architectural planning and plumbing, of laws of health and rules of Community life, three priests, a Brother, and eleven Sisters were lodged on the second floor, while five guards were at all times in residence on the first floor. Fortunately, the house had been a catechetical center, and there were two classrooms to the right of the stairway. These the priests and Brother took over. The eleven Sisters disposed themselves in four single bedrooms and the community room on the left. A hallway eight by fifteen feet was converted into a common room and workshop. Sister Sabina, Japanese and therefore free, approached the authorities. Sister Rachel reports the results:

> Sister explained to them that it was not customary for priests and Sisters to live under one roof. The response was, "We know you must have a priest for your religious observance, this is the only way we can provide it."

On the other hand, in Fushun, where the Sisters were interned in their own convent, no provision was made for a chaplain, though the rectory was but a couple hundred yards away. Sister Lelia writes:

> The Bishop and Fathers in the "West Yard" seemed to have a monopoly on all things religious; the Sisters for the first three months were without the consolation of the Sacramental Presence; for six months had no opportunity of going to confession in English. The thought of death seemed more than a remote possibility. Deprived of the Blessed Sacrament, with danger lurking at every turn, the Sisters went about their tasks serene and

unafraid, feeling more strongly than ever before that God in His Providence was watching over all. The Divine Office, the hours of prayer, day and night constituted our real activity, as never before.

In January, Sister Sabina arrived on business. She brought news of Dairen. Sister, popular with her own people, loved by the Sisters, diplomatic, far-seeing, with excellent judgment—had no difficulty in procuring a two-hour interview with Bishop Lane, escorted to the convent by his "protector," Mr. Mutota.

All the Sisters were assembled. It was at this time that the Bishop reminded us we had all the help we needed in an Act of Perfect Contrition. We can hardly hope to be as well prepared or as ready to die as we were then—but we were not considered worthy.

To the Japanese, the police are to some extent the representatives of the authority of the Emperor. This is the explanation of the obeisance which must be made to them. It is human nature that a wielder of such power at times acts as though he possesses it by right divine. Conflicting authorities complicated living. For example, in Hopei, restrictions were few. The Sisters continued their works of charity, sometimes assisted so far as supplies of food and coal went, by the police. They were even permitted to go to Honan, but one day an official there saw them and issued an interdict. It was confusing to find one could be both law-abiding and law-breaking at the same time! The official who particularly favored them knew a very little English of which he was inordinately proud. Sister Veronica Marie tells this story of him:

On one occasion while visiting us, he noticed our little portable organ. He asked one of us to play. A booklet of "Songs the World Sings" was handy. He made his own selection. So I played and he sang *God Save the King!* What's an enemy national anthem in the wilds of Manchukuo?

The Sisters recall him gratefully for, when Sister Paula was taken sick with what proved to be typhoid fever, he allowed a Sister-nurse to go from another house to attend, and later permitted an exchange of Sisters.

In T'ung Hua there was, likewise, authority divided against itself. The Sisters felt the repercussions. Late one afternoon they finished packing according to instruction their household effects in cupboards with locks and in trunks. As the last key was turned, a slightly more superior officer arrived who ordered everything unpacked, and repacked in boxes which he had to procure elsewhere.

The questionnaire was a perfected art with the Japanese long before the American student adopted the technique! Questions were the stock in trade of their police. No one who lived in Japan or her dependencies escaped them. Nothing was too personal, too intimate, too minute to escape attention. With war, the scope of investigation could not be broadened so its intensity was increased. At Dairen, in January, 1942, a formal inquisition was established. It may be used as an example of what all internees suffered—sometimes to a greater, at other times to a lesser degree. Sister Peter summarizes the six weeks it lasted:

The first day, it was Sister Gerard and I. The detectives asked where our rooms were and told us to go to them. I did not like the idea of being alone behind a closed door, and told the Sisters to stay close outside our rooms. I answered all questions in a loud voice so they could get an idea of what he was asking me.

I soon realized, this was to be a long drawn-out affair and explained to my questioner that being so closeted with any man was a serious breach in our code of etiquette, and asked for myself and for the other Sisters, that the inquisition be held in the public room. It took some explaining, but he acceded to my request. He explained the situation nicely to the man examining Sister Gerard, and thereafter, these seances were held in the community room.

The examination took hours and days, perhaps four hours at a sitting, and repeated for a week. Some of the questions had dangerous implications, so we never dared relax. As each one finished, her examiner read a summary of the interview and required a signature. By the time it was over every individual nerve fiber was worn fine.

Despite the complete dossier kept on every foreigner within

the boundaries of the kingdom, despite the times already asked and answered, each interview began with name, age, place of birth, parents, education. A college degree built on the firm foundation of a kindergarten beginning marked the holder as possessing greater latent powers than one who came to the degree from the first primary grade! Nights went either in worrying about one's next appearance or thinking of smart answers one might have made and didn't at the last session. Each interview ended with the promise—or was it threat?—of another one. It might come next day, it might be next week, but it was inevitable. Sister Stella Marie culls some typical questions and answers:

"What is your age—real and apparent?" I gave the same answer to each question. If he meant mental age, I wasn't going to give myself away!

"Why did you enter the Convent?" "To live a more perfect life."

"Well, don't you think we Japanese people can lead perfect lives?" "Yes."

"Who are your friends?" "All the people we serve." We never mentioned names.

"Do you love your country?" Patriotism is a virtue of religion for them. "Of course."

"Do you want to evacuate?" "No."

The exodus of all foreigners was devoutly wished for by the Japanese, but they did not want the odium of expelling religious.

"If you went home, you could help your country by Red Cross work, etc. So if you do not want to go home you are not patriotic." "We can pray for our country."

"Do you pray your country will win the war?" "I pray that the Will of God be done."

"Why are there countries?" There are times when I think Father Byrne's answer to all questions—"Original Sin"—is historically sound and very brain saving.

"What do you think of the Japanese guards?" "I don't think of them as a group—only of the one present."

"What do you think of the Emperor?" "Your papers say that he is a good man."

"If the Emperor ordered what the Church forbids, which would you obey?" "The Church is holy, if the Emperor is good he could not order what is not good."

"What do you think of the Japanese gods?" A very touchy subject! "I don't think of them."

"Is your faith perfect?" "I wish that it were."

Whenever we got stuck we fell back on the response, "The Will of God." Sister Sabina overheard one of the inquisitors complain to another one: "Those Maryknoll Sisters are very well educated but they are very simple minded—all they know is 'God, God, God.' " A lovely compliment, we thought, though not so meant.

All the time I was being interviewed I was worried sick whether or not I would get the local Christians in trouble, our Sisters and priests in the house, all Maryknoll or the whole Catholic Church.

Some of the inquisitors were just doing their job, but one chap had the fanaticism of a zealot and he did belabor the unfortunates who fell to his lot. How we prayed for them!

To an erstwhile Savoyard, the humor of Gilbert and Sullivan suddenly seemed grim:

> To sit in solemn silence in a dull, dark dock,
> In a pestilential prison, with a life-long lock,
> Awaiting the sensation of a short, sharp shock
> From a cheap and chippy chopper on a big black block.

At one of the missions, a Sister was undergoing routine questioning in the local police station when her medal of the Blessed Virgin, commonly known as the Miraculous Medal, aroused the attention of the gendarme. Eager to display his strictly rationed English, the Nipponese began to read the inscription on the medal—"O Mary conceived without sin. . . ." Suddenly, his eyes lighted up, and with the air of having unearthed a plot, he repeated exultantly—"O Mary conceived without sin, pray for—*United States!*"

Fortunately, the Sister was more proficient in Japanese than the officer was in English. She not only tactfully corrected his error, of mistaking the English word "us" for the abbreviation "U.S.," but took advantage of the opportunity to impart a doctrine lesson to a goodly number of listeners as well.

Not that life was completely without smiles or compensations!

In Dairen, one day, a shower threatened during the afternoon visit to church. The little congregation was at first startled and then amused when the yard monitor was heard to say to Sister Peter in a stage whisper, "It's going to rain, what shall we do about the wash?" Sister responded, "We'll be leaving church in a few minutes." When the Sisters went to the back yard, the man was taking down the frozen clothes. Courtesy to women is not an Eastern virtue. The Sisters believe Wada San's little act of kindness was patterned on the example of the Fathers and Brothers who were

most thoughtful, concerned for our welfare; kind and appreciative; unobtrusive but ready with their ministrations at the least hint; constructively helpful, caring for the Church, carrying coal, busy with hammers and nails and saws, giving us in its plentitude the richness of the Church's liturgy.

Sister Peter voices the tribute of the Sisters everywhere. In the white heat of suffering, the bonds that bind the Maryknoll Society and the Sisters Congregation have been tested—and they are good. It is the "oneness" that Father Founder and Mother Mary Joseph forged for their respective societies.

The story of Angie, by nickname, is Sister Peter's:

A new guard appeared one morning, a slim man in his early twenties. From the very first moment of his arrival he seemed genuinely interested in everything.

One day, he asked: "What is that?" pointing to the Miraculous Medal which we wear on a chain around our neck. I countered: "Have you ever heard of Christ?" He had not.

I went on to explain that Christ is the Son of the One, True God, Who took upon Himself our human nature and died on the cross to save us. "Mary is His Mother," I concluded.

He liked the explanation and handled the medal reverently. I asked him if he would wear one of these medals if I gave it to him. When his face brightened, I quickly added: "Will you wear two?" because I wanted very much to have him wear a medal of the Sacred Heart as well. "How shall I wear them?" was his next encouraging question.

I had no chain to offer him but told him my father and

brothers wore their medals pinned inside their coats and suggested that perhaps he should like to wear them in the same place. The whole experience was new to him. He opened his coat, and not knowing quite where to put them, I told him to pin the medals over his heart, secretly hoping that the love of Jesus and Mary would become part of him.

About a month later, he was on duty again and he scarcely signed himself in when he called me, flung open his coat and with a broad smile showed me the medals still there. He then asked if we had any books he might read about our Faith. I selected carefully those that would give him the best beginning —the catechism, a bible history, simple lives of the saints and a prayer book. For days he spent every spare minute reading them and whenever a companion guard seemed interested he shared the books with him. When he was replaced, he took the books along.

I have never seen this Japanese since, probably never shall, but by prayer am eager to give him more of the treasure that is ours.

The one provision that lacked variability was that of segregation. The guards were brusque, threatening, at times cruel, to the native Christians, who seemed to find some comfort in walking by the internment centers, and in attempting to share their little with the missioners. It was amusing, heartening, and frightening to see a tiny miss of six or seven, after a furtive survey of the field, dash to the back door—the bearer of gifts, a little sugar, a few eggs, a bit of meat spared from the family's scant larder! The internees had been permitted to pool the food resources of their respective convents when they came together. In Dairen they received a subsistence fee, wrung from the authorities by Sister Sabina. This was not the case at Fushun, nor elsewhere, and money needs and sleepless nights increased proportionately. As time passed, shortages increased. Every cook faced the need for a substitute raised to the nth degree. From the earliest days, the Sisters traditionally played the role of "Other Marys" to the Fathers. Of this facet of the Maryknoll vocation, Mother Mary Joseph wrote in 1936:

I like to recall that mine was the privilege of being the first of our Sisters to cook for the Seminary. Frightened by the isolation of the new Maryknoll, the cook had fled during the night, and a bewildered "father" of a cookless family called on us for help as soon as the desertion was realized. For a month, with the aid of some local talent, I had the joy of serving as Mary did, a household consecrated to God. From then on, whenever the need has arisen, our Sisters have in the spirit of Nazareth ministered in this way to the Maryknoll Society.

True daughters of their beloved Mother, the Sisters did everything in their power to assist the priests. Sister Lelia reports:

We washed and mended the Fathers' clothing; did the sacristy work, made altarbreads. We were able to eke out their larder, and sometimes to grace their table with some magic from our own kitchen.

When Bishop Lane and the Fathers were sent to Mukden, February 25, 1942, the Sisters were moved to the rectory. Word came back from the camp of a rigorous slenderizing diet. Sisters and laity combined to relieve the situation at least slightly. Sister Lelia continues:

Not only the Christians, but even the pagans whom we had helped at one time or another, donated money to buy liver, sugar, eggs and lard, that we might make cakes and cookies. Regular weekly trips were made by the former house boys, the cook, the catechists and parishioners with sweets for the internees. The Bishop listed fifty in his group. We found later, with his usual great-heartedness, he had included the Protestant missioners.

The Prince of the Church and the poor Chinese vying in Charity!

The Northern Lights were changing! The next signal would be "Go."

13

Carrying Their Sheaves

"UNLESS the grain of wheat falling into the ground die, itself remaineth alone. But if it die, it bringeth forth much fruit." These words come to me frequently. . . . Father General, of blessed memory, many times during the course of the years pointed out that unless we were humbled and apparently dead (to our selves), we would never make spiritual progress. So it is with our work. We see parts of it today, practically in ruins as far as the material end of things go . . . and now a number of Sisters are returning from certain missions because they are not free to work there any longer. All this is a part of God's design. In His permissive Will, He allows many seemingly adverse things to happen, which in the end are productive of much good. . . .

Our works are not dead! Only a part of them have been interrupted—temporarily. Our Sisters, uprooted from one place, are at home in another. Where souls are to be found, our Sisters are not strangers.

So Mother Mary Joseph spoke to the Sisters at the Motherhouse, August 14, 1942, while the "allied world" awaited word of the progress of the diplomatic ship, the *Gripsholm,* bringing in British, Canadian, and United States citizens from the Orient. Aboard were thirty-one Maryknoll Sisters. They were coming, somewhat as exiles, banished from their fields.

On December 8, 1941, Mother had written to the families of all the Sisters in the East:

Bishop Walsh has just returned from the Orient and he found the Sisters, wherever he saw them, in excellent spirits and in good health. Not one of them wished to return. Rather did they look upon running away from the flocks entrusted to their care as religious, as an act of desertion quite incompatible with their vocation. They love the people for whom they are working, whether they are Chinese or Japanese, Korean or Filipino and are ready to accept whatever God sends to them. This is a spirit I know you will rejoice in as much as I do. It removes from us a sense of fear that they are unhappy or where they would not be, a thought that is comforting to us all.

Reverend James Drought, Assistant to the Superior General of the Maryknoll Fathers, addressed a letter to Mother Mary Joseph, as follows:

MARYKNOLL
NEW YORK

April 24, 1942

Dear Mother:

The Holy Father, Pope Pius XI, desires that our Missioners should return home in event that negotiations are successful in effecting an exchange of American and Japanese internees.

With respect, therefore, to the disposition of our Missioners, our future policy has been decided for us by the Holy Father, and our Members can remain no longer provided arrangements for their repatriation can be effected.

Sincerely yours,

(Signed) JAMES DROUGHT

Rome had spoken. Communication from the center to the East was not possible. The Japanese brought pressure on the missioners to withdraw. Interned, they could not carry on their apostolate. The proper local ecclesiastical superiors assigned them back to the States. In some instances it took a long time before the orders could be fulfilled. Time is purely relative. Nowhere is this more true than in the Orient.

The Sisters from Korea were brought to Japan direct from their own convent in Yeng You. They arrived in the Land of the Rising Sun just after the famous flight of General Doolittle in the Spring of 1942. The surprise attack with its threat of a return visit was psychologically sound from the strategic point of view. Sister Gabriella thought it quite possible that the internees were used as Exhibition B—marched through the streets of Kobe, Tokyo, Yokohama, in lines, under police guard, counted, and roll called in public to give assurance to the people that the Government had matters in hand. Exhibit A, undoubtedly, was the riddled plane standing in the Japanese main square and placarded as one of the Doolittle armada. It is probable that this plane was authentic. But no internee accepted it as such. One of the anomalies of the war was that the repatriates received accurate information about its progress, and they believed not a word they heard.

The Fushun, Manchuria, missioners were taken by open truck, under guard from the Bishop's home, which had served as their camp, to the Club in Mukden, where Sisters Angela Marie and Miriam, and many Maryknoll Fathers, shepherded by Bishop Lane, were interned. Here they remained for six days. It is Sister Lelia who is chronicler for the travelers:

We had inspection of baggage, roll calls, and practice lining up with our baggage, until we wondered whether it was not army training we were having.

On the eve of our departure, the authorities gave us a *Sayonara* party—a regular meal, and with a bottle of beer for the men, one of cider for each lady! Speeches were in order. Basic English could not have borne the strain and delicacy needed for this. We shall never forget the talk given by Dr. Barker, Episcopalian president of the Mukden Seminary. It was his formidable task to give thanks to the powers that looked to our internment. The Doctor gave a litany of things for which he was grateful—the joy of a bath, the privilege of privacy ("not that I mind Father Haggerty who sleeps on one side of me; in fact I like him very much," said the scholarly doctor)—and, what made us internees of a week thrill with pride was the gracious yet earnest way in which he included Maryknollers in the litany. He was particularly grateful, he said, that the Japanese Government considered an old man like himself worthy of concentration, and more grateful that thus he had the privilege of observing "the great Church, which is the Mother of us all, through the daily life of its men and women!" Our separated brethren cheered him roundly. . . .

Later Maryknollers got together. The Bishop spoke to us, and we ended this last night together with *Maryknoll, My Maryknoll.*

> This is thy aim, thy sacred call
> To bring Christ's name and grace to all
> God speed thee on to save men's souls—

After the chanting of the Benedictus, we recited the prayer for travelers, and received the Bishop's blessing. It was a solemn moment!

Late the next afternoon, everyone assembled outside for a last handshake. That some of us did not know others seemed to matter not the slightest. It was the brotherhood of mankind! Shortly after seven, army trucks drove into the grounds for the evacuees. As we came to light on some piece of baggage for a seat, the Bishop started *God Bless America,* only we said "Columbia." The guards stood respectfully aside, and murmured "How these Christians love to sing hymns!" A remark to be heard again as we sang our way to Kobe through three nights, with not a chance to lie down. Some of the consular parties from Harbin and Mukden came from their coach to swell our choir.

On June 16, 1942, at the English Club in Kobe, our baggage was fine combed for the last time. Night saw us entrained for Tokyo—and a real American breakfast at the Station Hotel. A short train ride, a half hour, brought us to the boat, and we boarded the *Asama Maru,* only to ride at anchor for a whole week outside Tokyo Bay. Rumors were rife—despite the efforts of diplomats to be diplomatic, and newspaper men to be noncommittal. We were to be returned to internment; we were to be kept on the boat for the duration, *ad infinitum.* Then, on the twenty-fourth, in the early hours of the morning, orders were given and we sailed south for home by way of Hong Kong, Saigon, Singapore, Lourenco Marques, Rio.

It was at Singapore that the *Conte Verde* with Americans from Shanghai and vicinity joined the *Asama Maru.*

On July ninth, both vessels, electrically illuminated, with white crosses painted on the sides and under the Southern Cross which shone above, sailed on toward Africa—ten miles apart by night, five by day. They entered Lourenco Marques in Portuguese East Africa on the feast of St. Mary Magdalene, July twenty-second. The *Gripsholm* with her cargo of Japanese passengers had steamed into port two days before. The exchange of passengers was simply made, one to one, regardless of importance. For five days, we had the freedom of the city, Mass each morning at the Cathedral. If our hearts were not in Asia, Africa would have won them!

The difference in cleanliness, service, and food between the two boats was most striking. The first lunch on board the *Gripsholm* was a feast to the eyes as well as a temptation to appetites not yet keen. It was a buffet affair—laid out with chicken salad, sliced ham, potato salad, light white rolls and butter, ice cream, cake and pie; with shining silver, dainty china, and snowy linens. The scene was more Keatsian than Keats:

> Of candied apple, quince, and plum, and gourd;
> With jellies smoother than the creamy curd,
> And lucent syrups, tinct with cinnamon;
> Manna and dates, in argosy transferred
> From Fez; and spiced dainties. . . .
> On golden dishes and in baskets bright
> Of wreathed silver.

Living quarters on both boats were very crowded. The passenger list for *Gripsholm* accommodations was hopelessly confused. For the first two days after the exchange was made, confusion not unmixed with consternation reigned in regard to cabin accommodations.

When a group of Sisters offered to sleep on the floor of the cocktail lounge, the stewards were so grateful that they plied them with pitchers of lemonade and fresh oranges, and sat by looking on benignly, as the thirsty American Sisters made short work of the refreshments.

The second night, some of the Sisters were still cabinless. They waited patiently until the early hours of the morning as harassed officials tried to handle excited ladies. Finally, the Sisters told the man in charge they would be very comfortable for the night in chairs and not to worry about them. With that, the Captain, who was hovering in the background, stepped up to one of the Sisters, hand outstretched, and said, "Sister, I would like to shake hands with you and thank you. For this mix-up, we are not responsible." The Sister was so amazed that she shook hands like a solemn rite, then bolted.

American men have a chivalry toward women, which is not understandable to the Oriental, nor is it so marked in Europeans. Cheerfully and as a matter of course, the men took the poorer accommodations. This was a double sacrifice on the Japanese boat for while all paid the full fare, the food was according to class.

On board the *Asama Maru* and the *Gripsholm,* the Sisters were in great demand as teachers and nurses for children and grown folk; they took part in the musical programs, joined study classes, and made friends with all. One little child carried from the boat in the arms of the mother, tried to get free when she saw Sister Columba on the pier to greet the home comers. Her little arms were stretched out to be taken. She was accustomed to the Sisters and had confidence in every Maryknoll habit.

The ship carried many South Americans. In view of Maryknoll's new fields "south of the border," Sister Amata's remarks are interesting:

Aboard the repatriation ships, the people learned South American culture from the various diplomats returning to their countries from the Orient. In the course of the journey, the Protestants made statements to the effect that now that the Orient was closed to them as a mission field, they would devote their energies to South America. The South American diplomats, greatly incensed, announced publicly that they, Christians for centuries, had no need of proselytism. Vehemently declared Senor Iglesias, an energetic and charming gentleman from Chile, "all Latin-American people are Roman Catholic. Even the atheist —he is a Catholic."

The experiences of the Sisters on the two repatriation trips were much the same. In both instances the *Gripsholm* was the American ship. The Japanese *Teia Maru* replaced the *Asama Maru.* The course differed from the first, and in distance was greater. On September 14, 1943, the Sisters from Japan boarded the vessel. For one year short of a couple of days, Sister Gemma had been in the Sumire Camp, located between Tokyo and Yokohama, and ranking in infamy with Stanley Prison and Los Baños Camp. For that period, the ninety Sisters there were unable to go to confession, even when after many pleas over long weeks a chaplain was appointed to say Mass. Sister Gemma speaks glowingly of the work of the Swiss.

The Legation sent a representative to see us each month. The "official" was Father Hildebrand, a Swiss Benedictine, who with other Swiss nationals in Tokyo had been mobilized for the "duration" to help at the legation. He was indeed a friend. Everyone loved him. He was always accompanied by a "guardian" in the person of a high Japanese officer. This man knew English, and kept as close to Father as his shadow. Nevertheless, Father eked out our miserable larder by gifts of oatmeal, coffee (substitute), sometimes butter, jam—and books! May God ever bless the Swiss Legation for all it did for us!

Sister Gemma had worked with the Japanese a quarter of a century. "I have loved Japan," Sister says, "its poor and homey people, its cultured but distinctly minority group." Like all who know the race, Sister recognizes the inherent evils in militarism. The dream of supremacy is a dangerous one. The Jewish nation, in truth a Chosen People, was wayward, stiff-necked and proud. The false ideologies of a super-race and super-state have led astray some European nations. The Japanese cult of Emperor worship laid claim not only to a super-racial and super-national character, but a super-natural one!

In Kyoto, Sister Dolorita and Sister Camilla were interned in their own convent. They were able to have Mass in their chapel about once a week, and to go to the Church for Sunday Mass twice a month. When Father Byrne embarked on a Japanese-English language book, the Sisters collaborated sentence work and Father was permitted to go to the convent twice a month for consultation.

"I hesitate to put our little bit on paper. We had such an easy time of it. God has been so good," wrote Sister Camilla.

In less than a month after her arrival home, Sister died suddenly of an infection. Letters received from her ship companions stressed her complete unselfishness, her tireless devotion to the sick, her tact and humor with the over-worked and under-staffed ship personnel, her gaiety of spirit, which made her companionship so joyous.

Orders for repatriation of the Dairen community were for September 1, 1942. The second Exchange ship was to pick up the group at Shanghai. It did—a year later!

A *Missa Cantata* was sung in the Dairen Church on the day the missioners left. The Christians heard of the departure and they came to Church and walked in boldly. No one said them nay. There were many tears on the Communion plate that morning, Father Ryan told the Sisters. The people went to the dock and talked out their troubles there with their missioners. They stood on the shore and sadly watched the boat pull out. "Go away slowly, come back quickly," is an Oriental goodbye.

The Sisters were practically free in Shanghai for their first six months and they did an immense amount of catechetical work. They also organized the children at the American Relief Center where they lived, partly as a wholesome recreational feature, partly as an instructional activity, into a little theatre group. The long period of preparation for the Christmas play directed the thinking of these little folk "from scholastic trammels free," and gave occupation and interest. "Even the lovable, winning but impish Hanvy pair were reduced for moments at a time to simulate the strictly male angels they portrayed!" says Sister Luke. Adults offered to do constructive work. Mothers were happy to be costumers, fathers, stage hands. There was the Christmas Eve presentation followed in the next week by three *demand* performances. The Sisters found among the audience more than one who had never heard the sweet story of Bethlehem.

In Shanghai, the nine o'clock curfew ruled out midnight Mass. But in the Relief Center there was that privilege. The refectory was changed into a chapel, perfect to the last detail. The Religious of the Sacred Heart loaned their richest brocades, their finest altar fittings. Catholics in the city sent lilies until the entire room was banked with these exquisite blooms against an evergreen background. Everyone walked reverently, spoke softly throughout the whole evening—and at twelve Maryknoll's Father Ryan "went unto the altar of God"—and the crowded congregation—Catholic, Protestant, and Jew—felt once again the joy of their youth.

When the internment of civilians disrupted the American school, at the invitation of the school authorities, Father Ryan took over as principal and Sisters Gerard, Corita and Stella Marie supplemented the staff. They brought the children up to the eve of graduation. The day before the event, the Sisters were ordered to the Convent of the Sacred Heart, which had been designated as an assembly center for Sisters. The Religious of the Sacred Heart were wonderfully self-sacrificing, capable, valiant. The superior, Mother Neurey, was a real mother and she made the large family of ninety-nine assorted Sisters under her roof, one in the Heart of Christ. The internees wrought for the convent altar as a souvenir of their stay the most beautiful antependium that love could devise and skill produce.

On September 19, 1943 there was roll call and inspection of baggage at the convent, a quick farewell, a second inspection at the pier, a personal examination by an apologetic Chinese woman, and then the Exchange ship. The depths of charity the Sisters plumbed in that worldly city of Shanghai is a saga of brotherly love!

The *Teia Maru* dropped anchor at Hong Kong on the twenty-first of the month. Father Meyer, faithful to his care of souls in Stanley Prison, sent word by an internee from there that he would wave a white flag at four P.M. Hail and Farewell. San Fernando, Philippine Islands, was reached on September 24th. Saigon was the next port of call, thence to Singapore. On the evening of October 4th the ship sailed from Singapore. The route was through the Sunda Straits, across the equator twice, around the southern point of India, up the west side, many miles from the shore line, and into Mormugao, Portuguese India, on the Feast of St. Teresa—October 15th. The next day, the *Gripsholm* docked. Sister Peter recalling:

the *Ancient Mariner* felt very respectful toward the albatross which followed the ship and hoped no one would harm them.

Saturday afternoon, Mr. Langdon, who represents the United States Government on the Exchange Ship, visited the *Teia Maru*. "I have come to take you home," was his greeting to us. It was our first contact with America since 1941.

On Sunday the 17th, the Bishop of Goa called on the religious aboard.

The Sisters made every effort to visit the tomb of St. Francis Xavier at Goa, but without success. After a week in Mormugao, the *Gripsholm* sailed. This departure seemed to be signal for mail—the first any one had had in two years! Sisters Dolorita and Fabiola, on the 26th, joined some of the other passengers in helping with the typing of reports and official forms for the hard pressed officials. "Talkies" were new to many of the missioners. On both trips, the swimming pool was reserved for the Sisters at a given hour; this included steam baths, showers, and reducing machines. The last named were not needed. Sufficient slimming had been done in camps. It was all health giving, relaxing and normal.

The stop at Port Elizabeth, South Africa was a joyful experience. "We walked off the gangplank at about ten in the morning. It was the first time in two years we had been free citizens!" comments Sister Xavier Marie. The communities spent themselves in entertaining the religious. Some Maryknollers, including Sister Ellen Mary, visited the latter's cousin—a dear old Dominican Sister who had served in Africa for forty-four years!

It must have been an inspiring thing to hear the missioners sing, nightly, the *Ave Maris Stella*. Morning Masses were a problem for want of space. All the services were well attended—and by many who were not Catholic.

Rio de Janeiro welcomed the visitors. From the time the gang plank was put out, the Sisters were in the care of the Catholic Ladies of Brazil. Some went for a closer view of the *Christus Redemptor* atop the mountain. Others, who wanted to remember the first view of Christ standing with arms outstretched as if to welcome the wanderers from the sea lanes of the world, visited the various convents and places of historical interest. At six, the Archbishop greeted the group in the throne room; one of the priests, in his name, gave an address of welcome. Then His Grace received each one and gave his episcopal blessing.

One of the things that most impressed the Protestants was the universality of the Church as found in its members. At all ports, Sisters and priests, strangers but one in the Faith, met the boat and offered any service within their power to the missioners. On this subject Sister Peter says:

> The unity of the Church, rising above all national feelings saved the day for Catholic missioners in Manchuria. The Japanese authorities were fully aware that no move could be made that would not be reported to the Vatican and they were anxious to keep peace with the Holy Father. The Apostolic Delegate and Bishop Blois took over our interests in Manchuria as real brothers in Christ. We shall ever remember Bishop Blois's concern for us and our people—and his promise to hold everything in sacred trust until such a time as God saw fit to allow Maryknollers to return to the field.

The two trips from the Orient were made without mishap. It was hard to believe that the ocean itself was full of danger:

> On the eighteenth of August, we passed an empty raft and the derelict of a cargo vessel or a tanker, burned black and half sunk but with the eerie glow of a fire burning bright through the center. This was the most vivid, and practically the only gruesome reminder during the trip that we were never very far from a war of destruction on land, on sea, and in the air—

writes Sister Loyola.

The *Gripsholm* docked with her first load of repatriates on August 26, 1942. It took three days to check the passengers. Mother Mary Joseph spent those days, and into the darkness, on the pier, receiving each dear one as she was released. The boat made her second arrival on December 5, 1943 and was cleared practically in a day. The Sisters came ashore poised, radiant. They were thin, but not emaciated; their habits pressed, their bonnets in perfect condition, their linens immaculate. It must have taken them hours on line, waiting to get a chance to launder, to iron. These details may sound trivial, but they are part of that picture of mission Sisters, described by Archbishop Cushing in *New Horizons*:

> We lack the whole story of Catholic womanhood in the missionary tradition of the Catholic Church. For that story is one that evades tabulation and description. It is a hidden story. A story that keeps its own secrets in the hidden hearths of homes, of schools, of hospitals, of orphanages. For the flames that women tend are not the roaring fires that lay low whole continents for Christ, or devastate a pagan civilization. Women are skilled in tending tiny sparks; sparks that would flicker and die without careful nursing; feeble flames that glow and glimmer again in the warmth of encouragement; pale flames which burst at last into the molten heat that permeates perforce a pagan race—the hearth fires of the world.

In the beautiful Motherhouse chapel there rang out a great *Te Deum*. Above the chancel is the inscription "Gentiles shall walk in thy Light, and kings in the brightness of thy rising."

PART IV

Winter Wheat

14

These Are Our Jewels

"I HAVE never seen a stronger Christianity." Bishop Blois, the French Bishop of Mukden, a neighbor to the Fushun Vicariate, thus paid tribute to the Fushun Christians; to their courage, constancy, and absolute fearlessness in the face of real danger when carrying messages or going on other errands in the interests of the discredited American missioners.

Our hearts glowed with justifiable pride. These, our own people, who stood out as best among the good, had been commended by a man of a few words—one who had known their kind intimately for thirty years. We, on our part, had always felt that they were the stuff of which martyrs are made,

exults the Fushun Superior.

Rice Christians has been a term of reproach for convert work in Oriental fields. This war has shown the injustice of the criticism. Poverty in the Far East is something one cannot depict. It is not merely a lack; it is a tangible being of aggressive personality. And yet when funds were frozen, the priests and Sisters interned, and food supplies reduced to a minimum, these native Christians from the northern point of Manchuria down through the South of China, out of their little, alleviated the privations of the priests and Sisters. Sister Lelia tells that:

The day before Chinese New Year there was a knock at our back door. Who was there but our beloved Peter Souen. Very carefully he held in his hands a big dish of precious *Chiao Tzus,* or Chinese New Year meat pies. At the time food was scarce and meat almost unheard of. And Peter's convert father works for a pittance in the great open coal mines of Fushun.

"You should not have brought these to us," said Sister. "Your little brothers and sisters need them at home."

"Oh, no!" Peter answered, and smiled the captivating smile that made us his the very first time we saw him. "Ma said if each of us eats two less there will be enough for the Sisters."

Peter and the Sisters were friends. There had been an understanding between them since the day standing sturdily before them, little hands twisting his threadbare cap, he looked up into Sister Lelia's face and smiled. Peter was then in need but not homeless. He was a small but important member of the respectable but impoverished family of *Souen* living in *Ta Kuan Ting* (Big Official Place). Lured by the mirage of a land of plenty, the family had migrated from Shantung to Manchuria about five years before the war reached the outposts of that puppet state of Japan. Fushun, the city that boasts of the biggest open-cut coal mine in the world, was their destination, as it was for hundreds of others. It was a sad sight to watch the new arrivals herded together at the railroad station, waiting patiently for hours in long orderly lines to be led to the one-room company houses that they would henceforth call home. Not infrequently several families share one room. The most that could be said for the hovels was that they provided a poor place to sleep, and an uncertain roof overhead. But amid the inevitable squalor, the men and women rose with simple dignity to welcome all callers. Even though babies cried and children shouted, damp brushwood filled the rooms with smoke, and chill winds made entrance through the chinks—the long suffering miners and their families could be heard saying, "It can't be helped now. We must endure. But later—." And the Souens, bearing honorably one of the hundred common family names of the Middle Kingdom, struggled resignedly to "pass the days."

Malaria is inconsiderate of persons and conditions. One day late in August a frail little Chinese lady about thirty rapped hesitantly at the convent door. She explained haltingly:

In our *lao chia* [old country], we have a "Heavenly Lord's Hall" and the *tai fu* [doctor] is always ready to help the sick. My neighbors tell me that you do the same, so I've come for medicine for the "children's father" whose malaria is so bad that he can work no longer. The children are usually very good but now they are always whimpering that they can never "eat full" as they did before.

That day the Sisters visited the little shack, overflowing with family, but spotlessly clean. And some of the store from the convent shelves went along to help over the lean days. The younger members of the household peeped hesitantly at the foreigners from whatever distance they could attain in the small quarters. On subsequent calls the children made friends. They were overheard proclaiming contentedly to whoever would listen that there was a whole bag of sorghum and a basket of vegetables and soon, very soon, there would be even a piece of pork to season the main meal on the day of the Moon Festival. Mr. Souen had responded quickly to medication and was soon back in the mines.

Some months later Mrs. Souen, attended by her two sons and the baby girl, called on the Sisters. She said:

The "children's father" says that we must thank the Heavenly Lord for helping us in our trouble, so we have come to learn more about him. *Hsing-ma?* [Will it be all right?]

She had finished making over the family's padded winter clothes, winter shoes, and coverlets, so she would have a little free time. The Sisters arranged that she study the doctrine in the catechumenate during the day, the ten-year-old son in the school. If they persevered, the baby of two "borrowing the family's light" would be permitted to enter the church "free." The father sent word by his wife that he read characters and would study whenever time permitted. Then the question arose of the manly little chap of five years. Had he reached the use of reason? Some questioning, and the Sisters knew that he must enter his Father's House, not like the baby, but the hard way—via the study of the complicated Chinese picture-words, the characters of the catechism.

And he did, even though it took him two years; Mrs. Souen, her little daughter, no longer *Hsiao Nu* (Little Woman) but Telesa (Little Therese) and the older boy were Christians a whole year before Mr. Souen and *Hsiao Lien Tsu* (Little Chain) to be named Peter, were ready. They made most intelligent, faithful, fervent Catholics. Mr. Souen took the good tidings down into the bowels of the earth; what he learned of the Heavenly Lord he shared with his less fortunate companions. Mrs. Souen brought her neighbors to the convent. Joseph, the eldest son, was a good student, a dependable altar boy. Telesa at four would toddle over with her pagan friends, clutching a wilted bunch of dandelions for a shrine that caught her baby fancy.

But Peter! There grew up a perfect understanding between him and the Sisters he loved—he was their knight, their champion. And they were his friends. When the baby, a 'big joy' (boy) died, Peter eased the ache of his little heart to them. "Paul smiled twice before he died, Sister, do you think he saw his angel?" When war came, Peter was gruffly ordered by the police, "Don't have anything to do with the foreigners." Little Peter slipped in literally in the shadow of the guard. He bore some food sent from the family's scant supply, or a neatly corded bundle of kindling wood prepared by himself. In the spring, a friendlier guard was on duty, and he permitted some of the Christians to help the Sisters prepare and plant a garden. The Souen family reported together. The Father had taken a day off from the mines and lost a day's pay, in order to help. Peter spaded and planted, but his little soul strained for some means the better to express his devotion. It came. One of the Sisters admired his dog! That night his beloved pet joined the internees! It was arranged that Peter care for him by day. Each afternoon, the joy of sacrifice shining in his soft brown eyes, the little fellow strode whistling down to his alley home. Then the Sisters were removed to Mukden. The dog went back to his little master—but to him it did not compensate for the loss of his friends.

There was Mrs. Li who donated a half bottle of precious kerosene.

Sister: But can you spare it?

Mrs. Li: Oh yes, Sister, it's nothing to us. We go to bed earlier, and save the oil. My husband and I want to help keep the little lamp burning in the church."

On the Moon Festival, one of three big feasts of the year, the poor people were determined that since funds from the "beautiful country," as they call America, were not forthcoming, they must make up what was lacking.

We felt truly like little Sisters of the Poor—and we were in fact. For from their poverty, the Christians had brought us four live chickens, raised by the donors, a sack of rice, fruit and eggs. One of our parishioners gave an offering for a Mass for "the Sisters' spiritual and physical welfare." The following day, a seven-year-old dispensary patient brought three pounds of sugar (six persons' rations for a month) and smilingly assured us that "There's lots more at home—a whole half pound; anyway, we like salty things better!"

The police were forbidding, but the Chinese would watch their chance and dash in when they knew the guard was elsewhere. "You shouldn't be here," said Sister Eva to a lad. "Oh, that is all right, Sister, Lan has the guard arguing down the road."

Two native helpers went to jail because of their connection with the Americans. They were warned to have nothing more to do with the foreigners or they'd pay with their heads. This threat of extreme punishment was not an idle one. Others had suffered almost unto death for this crime. Father Pai, old and unwell, never recovered from the effects of his imprisonment. The American Fathers for whom he had suffered were permitted to attend his funeral, but were not allowed to commit to earth the fragile shell that had housed so great a soul. Father Pak, a

Korean priest, was taken and held for months in the loathsome, foul jail. Sister Rose of Lima describes him on his release:

He came to our convent; what a sorry sight! Bloated almost beyond recognition, vermin infested; clad in rough, native outfit, barefooted. A bichloride bath, clean clothes, a meal, helped his general condition. We managed to fit his small feet to the shoes of a big Sister. When he was ready to leave, we gave him one of our cloaks. With it flung around him, he looked a real curé. He went to the home of the Korean priest who had been sent to replace our Father. Next day, he had to present himself to the local authorities and thank them!

If these things happened to the priests, what chance had poor catechists! Nevertheless, released, the two immediately called at the convent. The guards, they had seen at the police station with Sister Elise and companion. "They can't be in both places." They countered logically the Sisters' orders that they depart!

Mission-arts, the industrial side of the Fushun mission, had a supply of materials, sewing machines, and tools. The Christians dismantled the machines; in sections they carried them out of the shop; rolls of materials they took off into safe keeping—until the day of the return of the missioners.

It was young Peter of the Smile who, when the Sisters were moved from Fushun to Mukden, negotiated a business deal. On the strength of his nine-year-old promise to repay, he borrowed a dollar and a half and made a trip to say goodbye. The tears in his eyes belied the smile on his lips as he reported: "The dog is lonesome. He won't eat since the Sisters went away." Was Peter ascribing to the animal his own big pain of separation?

Peter's Mother broke through the Bishop's guard one day just before the exodus. She, too, went to Mukden to say her goodbye. When she saw the Bishop, she fell on her knees—to kiss his ring reverently, as was her custom. But this time, she made a plea, "Please, Bishop, leave more of our Sisters with us." The Bishop walked away without responding—but Mrs. Souen knew that speech was beyond him of "the tender heart."

Of the last days at camp, Sister Lelia writes:

It was all very wonderful and quite heartbreaking at the same time. We had left Fushun, but Fushun had followed us. Every hour of the day more and more people poured in and stayed until the gates were closed. On the last day, they arrived in the early morning, and at noon, very reluctantly, went over to Madam St. Aidan's convent for a little rest and refreshment. They were with us to the end, even though armed guards stood between them and us on the Mukden station plaza.

None of these people thought of themselves as heroic, they were just informed by a fearlessness born of the Spirit.

With the freezing of accounts, the missions were often at a loss what to do. There were Church expenses, rent, teachers, catechists to be paid, charity cases, and more incidentals than one knew could turn up. At the Chinese church in Dairen, something drastic had to be done. It had been the custom there to take up a semi-annual collection—the people were desperately poor, and living conditions were becoming harder. Father Hewitt spent sleepless nights and worried days, and then decided to confide in his congregation. The missioners could manage to live, but could not support the church. Father tried to make it plain that he was talking to those who managed to eat regularly.

"Why did we not think of that ourselves? Father should not have to mention such things." The speaker was a new Christian, but one able to give. Father's plea brought in ¥2,000, a very large amount, and Father was visibly affected. Old man Li, who did odd jobs about the church for whatever Father could give him, happened to be in money. A debt owed to his dead son had just been paid—¥20. He halved it with Father. It was a sacrifice, for his wife was really sick. She died while the Sisters were interned. When Sister Fabiola was permitted to go to the convent on the eve of her departure for Shanghai, she met Mr. Li. "Sister, do you know? Now, only I, one person remains." His eyes were bright with tears.

Then there was a widow, also a Li, who had just been baptized with her five young daughters. She came from *San Pu Kuan,* a squatters' section between the railroad tracks. Even in China one's location in regard to the railroad seems to indicate social position. This poor widow gave her mite, ¥3. Whereupon her shack was robbed of the bit of winter clothing she had, and much worse, of her ration book which was in the coat pocket—and the law was inflexible—"No ration book, no eat!" She went to Mass next morning, shivering without her ragged wrap. When she returned home, she found the "Good Thief" had thrown the ration card back into her yard!

In Dairen, when the priests were interned, the Church was left without a leader. At no time would the Bishop of Mukden be in a position to take complete care of the Fushun Vicariate, of which Dairen is a part. Sister Fabiola tells of the Christians' handling of the situation and of Lao Meng:

> The priests were disconsolate about this; but there were a few influential men among the Japanese Christians who they thought might go surety for Father Ryan and prevail on the police to allow him to say Mass for the Japanese on Sunday—the police—of course, to be present. They were less optimistic about Father Hewitt's or Father Lenahan's being permitted to go to the Chinese Church. . . .
>
> Among the men who had always taken a prominent part in the affairs of the Japanese Church were Mr. Oka, principal of one of the high schools, who had a son studying for the priesthood, Mr. Sato, Judge Yasuda, and Mr. Akatsuke. Who was the moving factor, I do not know, but these men formed a committee with an equal number of Chinese Christians to handle Catholic affairs in Dairen. As none of the Japanese spoke Chinese, and none of the latter spoke Japanese, Lao Meng who spoke both tongues fluently was appointed interpreter. Lao Meng was attractive and capable; with the ease of one born in the Church, she proved a most able intercessor as well as interpreter.
>
> The committee couldn't get all they wanted, but they got more than they really hoped for. They knew the local set-up, army and navy versus local police, departments versus departments, and they knew it to be in the realm of the impossible to get all to agree on all points. The priests were not permitted to say Mass, hear confessions, or communicate the Christians. As a matter of fact, Father Lenahan tried out one day, walking calmly to the confessional—nothing occurred. So confessions in the Church were not scheduled, but occasionally took place. In fact, the committee secured permission to have weddings sol-

emnized at Mass and to have the priest, accompanied by a detective, go on sick calls. Father Ryan officiated at about three marriages during internment. To do this, the police had to be notified in advance and the request approved, after which Father Ryan received official notification. We were glad that Mr. Sato's daughter was the first to benefit by the work of her father.

The day of a wedding, the compound buzzed with detectives —not guarding valuable jewels, but seeing that nothing untoward might happen to offend the Majesty of the Emperor deity. We managed discreet peeks from upstairs windows, and we knew what the well-dressed bride wore in war time, how scared the groom looked, who were the guests. The Christians expected us to be watching, and many a covert wave was directed toward the house.

Lao Meng thought they had done well, but she did not rest content. She went to Mukden to beg the French Bishop to send a priest to Dairen. Bishop Blois was already overwhelmed trying to staff the Fushun Vicariate, but he recognized the need as pleaded by Lao Meng. He sent Father Pi, first once a month, and later appointed him pastor of Dairen. To see the Japanese bow in Christian submission before the priestly authority of the Chinese pastor was beautiful evidence of the unity of the Faith.

Each group took the financial responsibility for its church. If we seem to stress the work of the Chinese in this regard, it is because the people were much poorer and the sacrifices correspondingly greater. The Chinese church was a rented building; the people pledged themselves to take care of the rent. They did more; they helped support the pastor; they paid salaries to three girl catechists; they kept the catechist Lou Hsein Sheng. He had been offered an opportunity to better his financial condition, but it did not seem even a temptation to him. What the committee could pay, he accepted—he realized so fully that not by bread alone does man live, himself or another.

This Lao Meng, the interpreter, admired and trusted by both the Japanese and the Chinese members of the Church committee, was a real personage, and she had earned the confidence of all Christians by her way of life. A linguist of ability, speaking Japanese well, and expressing herself with the greatest ease in choice Mandarin and in Formosan, there was yet mystery in her failure to master English, even after seven years study. She wore English clothes well, a distinction for an Oriental woman. Herself a Chinese, she had married a Formosan doctor, whom she had the privilege of baptizing on his death bed. He was stricken suddenly; probably the malady was meningitis. Earlier, with his permission, his wife and four children had entered the Church. This was a concession, as two of the children were boys. He too was interested in the Church, but had not quite the courage to brave the maternal wrath.

Lao Meng admitted that at one time Doctor Meng had spoken of taking a second wife, one of the nurses in the hospital where he had been attached. This was quite an ordinary procedure among men of his class, so Lao Meng reluctantly consented. Her father had done the same thing, so no matter how she might dislike it, the idea was not shocking. Then came Lao Meng's Baptism. Later the doctor confided to her, "I'm glad the affair did not come off because, since we have known Jesus, it wouldn't have seemed right." Certainly the doctor was in good disposition for the saving waters of Baptism.

One morning Father Hewitt received a telephone call.

"I have just baptized Meng Hsien Sheng: he is so much worse, and I'm afraid I did not do it right."

"Just what did you do?" asked Father.

"I poured water on his head, and while I was pouring it, I said, 'Saint Joseph, I baptize you in the name of the Father and of the Son and of the Holy Ghost."

"He is validly baptized then, if he wanted to be," Father assured her. He didn't even mention the fact that her canonization of her husband was a bit premature—not much perhaps, for the good doctor died that night.

The funeral of so prominent a man presented difficulties. Lao Meng sought Father's advice, and he loaned her Lou Hsein Sheng, his catechist. A task for which Lou was just suited, said Sister Fabiola:

He would have a deep sympathy for Lao Meng and a thorough understanding of intricacies of her position. He would know what could be done to gratify the pagan relatives and what must be dispensed with to keep the integrity of the Catholic doctrine. He would be an ideal Master of Ceremonies and all who met him would appreciate the soul that looked forth kindly and fearlessly from behind the thick lenses of his glasses. They would know he was a scholar and accord him an instinctive respect. It was better though that the doctor's mother was in Formosa, a safe seven or eight days away. It happened that Bishop Lane was in Dairen and he offered the Mass of Requiem.

Lao Meng was not only head of the little family but also bread winner. She took over the doctor's X-ray work, but managed to keep up her visits to the poor in the hospital. It was in listening to her conversation with a patient that the Sisters learned that for seven years Lao Meng had waited patiently for the consent of her husband to enter the church—the seven years she had played at studying English—a means of contact with the Sisters!

In the Church in China, Lao Meng stands out as a valiant woman, and the mother of Christians—two stalwart young sons, and three beautiful daughters. Mary Magdalen, the baby, born shortly after the father's death, grows more to his image with each passing day.

Law abiding citizens—Korean, Manchurian, Chinese, Japanese, they risked liberty, and at times life, to provide for the missioners. Some delighted in devising ways in which to carry in food. Eggs, precious as diamonds, traveled in strange containers. One old lady had her cloak lined with pockets, like sticks, in which she carried her supply. House boys, almost under the eyes of the guard, threw supplies, not approved in the order, across a fence, and then appeared for inspection of the basket. One shopkeeper offered the Sisters an account, payable after the war.

In Kowloontong at the Maryknoll Convent School, Chaw Kwai, faithful old amah, resented the soldiers 'borrowing' the Sisters' blue tea set, and much to their dismay, she went to the officers' quarters and got it! Sister Matthew Marie expected the third battle of the Marne to burst before noon, but nothing happened. Perhaps the Japanese recognized when they were beaten—or they might have found a silver set!

A Lan had "taking ways" and her services at the convent had been dispensed with. After the fall of Hong Kong she called on Sister Paul. She had some tomatoes grown in her own garden! She became the Sisters' purchasing agent—and most faithful was she. Some friends from Kowloon, and A Lan would don coolie outfits and walk twenty miles to Uen Long, a market town in the New Territories. Next day they would retrace the weary miles and sell their food stuff at a few cents profit. This kept up until the Japanese intercepted them and leveled a penalizing tax on their enterprise. Former school girls reduced to want, vestment workers in dire poverty, tried to do something for the Sisters, some milk, a half measure of grain, and one a rose! "If thou hast two loaves of bread, sell one and buy a hyacinth to feed thy soul" runs a Persian proverb. The blossom spent its life on the makeshift altar in the basement shelter.

The younger missioners declare that Fah Wong, the convent caretaker, is an ex-bandit turned Christian. The toughness of his character is scarcely sufficient proof of their claim. But strong he is, in a moral sense, for the poor body is withered and wraithlike. He constituted himself Protector Number 2 of the Sisters, during the Japanese occupation. First place he ceded only to Father Feeney. The motto of the Netherlands *Je maintiendrai* was unknown to him, but the one night Father Feeney was away from the convent Fah Wong's bearing as he placed his mat across the doorway to the Sisters' shelter, declared "I will maintain." And he did through the long days, though he knew what it was to be brought to his knees at the point of a bayonet!

Mooi Kwai was born a Catholic. For a long time the Sisters doubted if she would have been one otherwise, she seemed definitely allergic to exertion, manual or mental. Even her Catholicism she exercised only enough to keep within the law, not with grace abounding. She came from a small city, where her father was a storekeeper. Merchandising is a lucrative business in China. Despite the fact of his comparative well being, the father was set on Mooi Kwai going to Kowloontong to work in the industrial department run by the Sisters. The girl was not altogether eligible, as the work strictly speaking was to help needy girls earn a decent livelihood. The Sisters would have been glad to escape excepting on this technicality but they permitted themselves to be persuaded by the earnest plea of the parent and on the recommendation of the clergy, and for the next two years they were very sorry they had not stood firm in their refusal. Mooi Kwai means Rose, and this one's thorns of laziness and carelessness pricked Sister Liguori and Sister Maria Teresa, distressed the diligent A Hing, and were somewhat hard on lovely brocades, and satins, and silks. Reprimands the Briar Rose shed as summer's dew. It was not an easy matter to return her to her father, for such an action meant loss of face, a truly serious matter. Sister Maria Teresa is Chinese but in her days in the States she culled some Americanisms which she brings forth usually incorrectly on the right occasion. In discussing the problem child with Sister Liguori she agreed that the father knew what he was doing when he dispatched her to the big city. "He was slipping the duck, Sister, that's what he was doing, just slipping the duck." Some hours later it came to Sister Liguori "passing the buck" was the expression the little Oriental Sister was unconsciously paraphrasing. Rose was far from languishing when the war caught up with her. The girls lived in a dormitory not too far from the industrial rooms, under the direct chaperonage of A Nap and the more remote control of Sister Maria Teresa. With the beginning of hostilities, the girls were on their own. The Sisters worried about them, particularly about Mooi Kwai. Then small containers of milk began to appear at the convent. It was most welcome but who was the generous benefactor? With the fall of Kowloon friends began to drop in occasionally but Mooi Kwai was a daily visitor. Then the Sisters discovered that Rose had a dairy job. She asked that a part of her poor pay be in milk and it was this she was leaving at the convent. With difficulty she was persuaded that she must accept pay for it. "The uses of adversity!"

The story of the Christians everywhere is one of unswerving fidelity to their priests and Sisters. Every returned missioner has a favorite tale of his Oriental "jewels." These are but a few, selected almost at random. May they shine for all Eternity!

15

More Precious than Rubies

MARYKNOLL'S Founding Fathers and Mother—hewed strictly to the principle of service of God, in His Church, *according to the Mind of the Church.* Thence followed two corollaries: the Church being Universal, the obligation of Maryknoll missioners is to Christianize, not Americanize, the people of other lands. The second deduction is implicit in the familiar phrase, *The Maryknoll Movement*—for so long as there is a pagan field, Maryknoll has no fixed abiding place. Individual Maryknollers may, it is true, spend a life time in one field, but Church History works in eras larger than the normal span of man's working years. The Mind of the Church is that everywhere native vocations to the priesthood and Sisterhood be nurtured; and that, as soon as is prudent, a native hierarchy be established.

The wisdom of Mother Church in raising up a native clergy was particularly evident in the occupied territories of the Far East. *The Field Afar* for February, 1943, records:

> In China there are twenty native bishops, and over two thousand native priests. . . . It is difficult to estimate how many of these native clergy are in occupied areas, but it is a tremendous guarantee of the continuance of religion that even a small number should be there ministering to the needs of souls and keeping alive the flame of faith.
>
> Over seven thousand daughters of the Orient are now working among the millions of afflicted men, women, and children in their own land.

Apropos of the life of the Church is the story Sister Lelia tells of Hou Telesa's brother. He was told that the vestment-making shop at the Fushun mission was closed, and he protested energetically:

"Don't tell me that the industrial room is closed. Don't I know that the Church is not extinguishable and can never die?"

The little lad might have been confusing the indestructibility of the Church with mere passing phases of Her activity.

"Or did he have vision?" one queries. The Church is not dead. The seed has been sown. It is being watered with the tears, possibly with the blood of the native clergy. Shall we be there for the harvest? For us, earth could hold no greater joy! What really matters is that there be a harvest, with native priests and Sisters in the fields for the reaping!

From earliest days, the Sisters accepted into their Congregation Oriental girls. The selection is based strictly on qualities which mark a vocation as *foreign mission,* and on the opportunities that can be provided for that vocation to function. And God works in devious ways! For over two decades, Maryknoll labored among the Japanese in California and in the State of Washington. Fine groups of Americans of Japanese ancestry, educated in democratic principles, had entered upon the American way of life. Then came Pearl Harbor. There were several Japanese Sisters on the west coast at the time. The Government granted permission for them to return to the Maryknoll Motherhouse, under the guardianship of Mother Mary Joseph. When it was decreed that all others be interned, Maryknoll hoped to move her little Christian groups intact into assigned camps, with priests to minister to their spiritual needs, and Sisters to carry on the education of the young. This privilege was not granted. It was then that Sister Susanna and Sister Bernadette asked to go as internees to Manzanar with their people. If any queried then "What are two among so many?" the records of their four years of service reproach "Ye of little faith."

On the other hand, under the direction of the Bishops, Maryknoll Sisters fostered over a period of long years—native communities in South China, Manchuria, Korea, and Japan. When the war came, there were seven such communities under their care. The first Sisters of Bishop Paschang's Congregation of The Immaculate Heart of Mary, five in number, were professed on the feast of Our Lady of Lourdes, 1936. Their training took ten years; begun in Kowloon, it was finished in Kongmoon. Two and two, the newly professed went to their mission stations just before the Japanese invaded their country. When Bishop Paschang was escorted by Japanese troops to Macao, His Excellency instructed the missioner left in charge of the Vicariate:

> The one point upon which I wish to insist is that the group of young women who are preparing for our Chinese Sisterhood be kept intact and at their task, no matter what other sacrifices must be made. For the very reason that the future is overcast with doubt, we must realize that the heart of our task lies in strengthening the Church's Chinese forces in these days as thoroughly as possible.

At the Korean Mission in Heijo, internment depleted but did not wipe out the clerical forces. Missioners of neutral countries and those from Germany and Italy were permitted to function. In some places the French priests were free agents. Native priests could also perform their sacred ministry—not unhampered, however, and particularly if they had worked closely with the Americans. The Heijo Vicariate had eight native priests. In the first days of the war, four of the number were arrested; three were imprisoned for over two months and the fourth for over four months. But the native Bishop of Seoul zealously assigned four of his own priests to the Maryknoll district.

In Heijo, Sister Agneta, a choice daughter of the Land of the Morning Brightness, was in charge of the native Sisters of Our Lady of Perpetual Help. This congregation was fairly well established. By 1941, twenty Sisters had been professed. When Maryknollers were interned and later repatriated, little groups of these Sisters took over the various mission houses. In this way the vacant convents were not an invitation to the Japanese to confiscate. Too, the native Sisters would be able to do much to sustain the little Christianities.

Sister Agneta, though Korean, dressed in the Maryknoll garb was classified as "enemy alien" and her movements restricted. "The cowl does not make the monk." This was exemplified in Sister's case. Never was she so truly a Maryknoller as when she donned the habit of the native Sisters, for the duration. Only then was Sister Agneta free to act—for the good of the people, and to assist Maryknollers. No trip was too arduous to take, no red tape too tedious to unravel to obtain a permission. In a great measure Sister Agneta's was the authentic voice of Maryknoll in Korea. It was Sister Agneta who carried to the Bishop in Seoul, Bishop O'Shea's account of affairs in the Heijo Vicariate; it was Sister Agneta, who contrived ways and means to keep in touch with the Sisters interned at Yeng You and Shingishu; it was Sister Agneta who managed to eke out supplies, as, now salt, again flour or sugar, ran low; it was Sister Agneta who twice wangled permission from the authorities for her to visit Yeng You and to remain overnight; it was Sister Agneta who visited the City Hall at Heijo when evacuation of Americans was settled, and arranged that Maryknoll convents and their appurtenances be turned over to Our Lady of Perpetual Help Sisters. It is Sister Agneta who carries upon her not-too-strong shoulders the burden of Maryknoll's mission work, dividing the activities among the native Sisters and directing its performance. These little Sisters have great affection for Sister Agneta. The Japanese authorities showed amazement at the perfection of her Japanese speech and respect for her dignity; nor did they fail to recognize her sagacity. Sister knew exactly what could be done and politely persisted until her requests were granted. On the other hand her demands were always reasonable. "Cut off from her own community, Sister feels the loneliness; but she is doing a valiant work," says Sister Eugenia.

There was no Maryknoll Manchu Sister to take over the direction of the Chinese Sacred Heart Sisters in Fushun, nor had there been a profession in the Congregation. But Bishop Blois in this matter, too, came to the help of his sister vicariate. He brought to Mukden the novices, and before the Maryknollers withdrew from their mission territory two groups of native sisters had finished the long probationary period, were professed, and installed in the Fushun convents, where they were carrying on the doctrinal instruction classes. The compounds once again buzzed with mission activities—this time with natives taking the lead.

While there was much that was pathetic, there was something prophetic, thought Sister Rose Benigna, as the bus taking the American Sisters into internment pulled away from the Maryknoll Academy in Dairen. She looked back to Sister Sabina, Japanese, fragile, wind blown, snow covered, standing erect and composed—for the sake of those who were going and for the two native women standing on either side of her. As her vision dimmed—by distance and unshed tears, Sister Rose Benigna saw Sister Sabina turn to comfort her companions. Lao Che had dissolved in tears, an unusual display of emotion for an Oriental, as "topside Missy" (Sister Rose Benigna, Superior) and the other "Sidders" told her a hasty and grateful farewell. Furuyu San, the Japanese teacher, remained as companion to Sister Sabina. With the help of two Russian girls, graduates from the academy, and Furuyu San, all converts, Sister Sabina kept the school running. It was still in operation, when after V-J Day some G.I.'s penetrated to this Northern city, newly come under Russian domination. To the soldiers, the Swiss Consul's daughter sturdily declared—"I learned American"—from this polyglot group!

Sister Peter pays tribute to Sister Sabina:

In spite of a frail physique, she was magnificent! Her wisdom, courage, control, resourcefulness, and entire disregard of herself made her an example I hope never to forget. We wondered how so fragile a body could support so great a soul.

With the officers she was absolutely fearless—always reaching out for opportunities to explain the Catholic position and the meaning of our religious life. Others who heard her at the

Foreign Office of the Provincial Government say that she "confessed" convincingly and in a very acceptable way her place among us, and our foreign mission vocation—explaining our form of life and our need of privacy for silence and meditation.

Mr. Hashimoto, chief of the Foreign Office, told me that he was beginning to understand us very well through Sister Sabina's explanations. I know he respected her highly.

Even with less friendly officers, her tact and gentleness won her point.

Twice she took distant trips to Shinkgo in our behalf. Twice she made the long ride to Fushun to consult Bishop Lane, and to see our Sisters interned there.

On the morning of September 1, 1942, when we Maryknollers were being taken to Shanghai under guard, Sisters Sabina, Talitha, and Elise were not permitted to go to the boat. They accepted this deprivation wonderfully though their hearts were breaking.

Sister Sabina's last words were: "Give my love to Mother. Tell her we will do all we can to keep the Maryknoll spark alive here. Don't let them forget us. We are Maryknollers, too."

Of the trinity of Maryknollers—nationals—outside the camp Sister Peter says:

Our "externs"—Sisters Sabina, Talitha and Elise—gave proof of a beautiful union among them, of deep affection to us, of consecrated devotion to the Church. They kept the school going, attended the hospital calls, carried on choir rehearsals, continued instructions to the adults and children at the Japanese mission. In addition, at Father Hewitt's request, they visited his Chinese mission, encouraged and edified his people.

On Sundays, when a priest from the Mukden Vicariate came for Mass, the three Sisters fasted for the ten o'clock Mass, then gave catechism instruction, rehearsed the choir, cared for the altar, visited among the people, and then trudged back home two miles to prepare their meal. And this in all kinds of winter weather and always with the worry of trying to support themselves and purchase food in a city suffering from a food shortage!

Sister Rose Ann is, among our Sisters, the most thoroughly modern edition of Japanese womanhood. Her face is more revealing; her speech more expressive; her cast of thought more original; her humor more spontaneous; her sense of adventure more daring. Born in Japan, she was converted in Seattle, took her degree at Catholic University, in the District of Columbia, was professed a Maryknoll Sister in New York and returned to do apostolic work in her own land. When war broke, she and Sister Gemma were training native novices in Tokyo. Sister Gemma went to Sumire Camp and Sister Rose Ann to Dairen, but not before she visited the Sisters held in Kobe awaiting the repatriation ship, *Gripsholm*. To effect this brief meeting, Sister donned native dress. The rich brocaded costumes that had made any Japanese gathering a rich tapestry of color, were banned during this time of national trial. Garbed in graceful kimono of dark gray, the slightly modified sleeves edged in blue, with a butterfly obi of the same hue, holding an authentic pass from the Japanese authorities, a gracious but not too interested lady of position, she would pay her respects to American friends! Sister's time was limited, conversation in the presence of a guard purported to understand English had to be circumspect; but her delicate little face told of suffering at being unable to help her Sisters. The exiles sailed away with a remembrance of the abiding Faith that shone in her eyes, a realization of the moral and physical courage required to make the contact, and a conviction that while they had sowed—there were others left for the reaping.

Sister Peter gives testimony of a like fidelity among Oriental Sisters of other communities working in the East.

During our internment at Shanghai and on the boat, I often talked with Sisters from other communities who had to leave native Sisters. I spoke to Notre Dame Sisters who have subjects in China and Japan; to Sacred Heart Mothers whose big schools were taken over by their native Nuns; to Franciscans, Loretto Sisters, and the Franciscan Missionaries of Mary—and all of them spoke in the highest terms of their native Sisters—their courage, good sense, and spiritual strength.

It must be remembered that these Sisters were loyal to their own countries but they held a clear distinction between Church and State. They seemed to have a special sensitiveness for the things that are God's; and to their land, they were ready to give the things that belong to Caesar.

In the more spacious days of peace, talking price was an entertaining pastime in China. No vendor expected to close a deal on a first offer. He would not only be surprised, he would feel deprived of his lawful right to argue. The serenity of China is that of the sage, not the mark of the man of business—be he pedlar or merchant. If Sister Maria Teresa is a philosopher, she is one who knows well her countrymen.

"If I give you all that rice for such a miserable sum, I shall be beggared," the old one presiding at the food stall cries, but he essays a sly wink at Sister Maria Teresa's companion, an American Sister.

"Well, our religion teaches it is hard for the rich to enter the kingdom of heaven," counters Sister with the umost equanimity. Then as an afterthought—"Have you any children?"

"My sons were killed in the war." The old man's face grows wistful.

"There are over four hundred children in our home," Sister suggests.

"You win, you win! In memory of my boys I will give you the food to raise up other sons for China. But you will make a beggar of me yet." The scene is enacted almost daily. The old man argues, only to give in.

"When you are poor you can come and live in our refuge," Sister promises as with a bright smile she picks up a heavy load and starts for the orphanage.

Sister Maria Teresa was the only Chinese among the five nationals left in the Maryknoll Convent when the Americans went to Stanley. Later, she left Hong Kong with Sister Paul, over the route that many of her compatriots had taken through the long months—to Macao. And there she remained using her every energy to alleviate the suffering of exile, family separations, and gaunt poverty that was the lot of the refugees. That her ceaseless activity and the pain of sympathy wore down her strength is not a matter for surprise. Sister Patricia, who developed

Maryknoll's work amongst the homeless in Macao, gives a pen picture:

Besides the children's home, we have a near-by refuge for almost a thousand beggars, whom we visit twice daily. In a single month we baptized ninety-five dying people at this refuge. Another of our tasks is to give one meal daily to five hundred refugees for whom we have no room in our shelters.

Sister Maria Teresa loves children and manages them beautifully. She supervises all the cooking and does the marketing, finds time to see that the dormitories are kept spotless, to help with the livestock, and in the vegetable patch.

Later, she insists on visiting the refuge, although it is not her turn. "A girl who is dying there feels very bitter," she explains. "I have thought of how I may comfort her and give her faith."

At last the children have been safely tucked in, and we have gone to bed. I am dozing off, when I hear Sister Maria Teresa stirring about.

"What is the matter?"

"I just remembered something I want to put out for breakfast," she says. "Then, that little girl who was brought to us today is probably frightened. I'm going to sit with her a while. Now for goodness' sake, don't worry about me. I'll be back before you know it!"

When peace came, Sister Maria Teresa returned immediately to Kowloon. There, despite broken health, she awaited the refugees, welcomed them home, and now enheartens them as they rebuild a new life!

16

The End Is My Beginning

"THE cup which cheereth, how goodly it is," thought Sister Frederica. It was the supper line-up, the first meal for the Los Baños internees within the American Camp at Muntinlupa. One of the paratroopers with the Eleventh Air-borne Division saw Sister. They were old friends, counted not in time but in experience. He was one who had fluttered from the sky that morning in February of 1945 and had effected the deliverance of the civilian prisoners. Sister had, during the melee, given him a drink of what passed currently as coffee in Los Baños. Now, he broke away from his companions, walked over to her with his canteen cup of steaming coffee in hand, and as he passed it to her he remarked with emphasis—"This is the real thing!" Sister tells the story:

No knight of old proffered the beaker with courtlier air! I accepted the cup so gladly. Its fragrant contents I shared with many tired persons in the line. We were one large family. The husband held the vessel to the lips of his wife, she gave it to the weary youngsters in turn, and finally I had it back. I recalled the famous wine cup ceremony of the Igorotes. At Tublay we had taken part—putting our lips to the cup that had made the round of the gathering. Not to do so would have offended. As a nurse, my antiseptic soul had protested. Tomorrow it would be again in the ascendancy—*but* today—every man was my other self.

Since the moment of release, the Sisters were on their way to Manila—the first of Maryknoll's displaced contingent in the Orient to start the trek back to the missions. Muntinlupa was but a halting place en route.

. . . think not much of my delay
I am already on the way,

. . . . . .

Each minute is a short degree,
And every hour a step toward thee.
At night when I betake to rest,
Next morn I rise nearer . . .
. . . almost by eight hours sail,
Than when sleep breath'd his drowsy gale.*

Muntinlupa was designed for a prison, hence it did not lend itself to conventual seclusion. What it lacked in privacy, it more than compensated for in the warmth of hospitality and the solicitous care it gave each refugee.

Grandma might call it carnal, but the Sisters' reaction to good food was a promise of their own well-being and was reassuring to those back home. Sister Maura Shaun writes:

We are being served by the Army three times a day in the chow line, with a daily issue of candy, cookies, cigarettes. It's all genuine American production. Some people, that is even 80%, are suffering an unpleasant reaction to the high protein diet, but there is no complaint about *that*. The Army kitchen tries to feed us as our mothers would if they were here; then the Army doctors treat the swollen lips and sore throats with sympathy, at the same time telling the patients to keep right on eating all they get; and the Army nurses have untiring strength and energy when it comes to caring for us all.

Sister Ancilla Marie has long, long thoughts:

I doubt if I can ever take a piece of bread for granted again! It takes the experience of the last three years, and especially the past four months, to realize God's goodness—and my "thank you" for the necessities of life are a bit more fervent than formerly.

A great public act of Thanksgiving for deliverance was the Solemn Mass offered on March 7, 1945, in Muntinlupa. It was fitting that the day was the feast of a great Dominican, St.

* Henry King: "The Exequy."

Thomas, for the history of the spiritual and cultural development of the Philippines is one with the glorious story of the Order of Preachers in the Islands.

Unaware of the correspondents' picture of G. I. Joe, the refugees draw the same attractive fighting lad:

> Of course he is big, muscular, a fine specimen of manhood, but the thing that is impressive and makes us love him is his gentleness, courtesy, consideration, tenderness toward us. The foreigners in our midst are overwhelmed!

So speaks Father Russell Hughes. Sister Marcella writes:

> There are thousands of soldiers here, and from nearby camps come others who walk miles to talk to the first white civilians they have seen in the years of the campaigns in Hollandia, Admiralty, Leyte. Some came in hot from battle, and delight us with their immediate surrender to the little internee children who are getting their first of common things—potatoes, movies, cornflakes, and *jeeps!*

"Wherever one finds a group of little ones, an American soldier is sure to be in the midst of them" has become axiomatic over the whole fighting world. Sister Rose Catherine describes the scene:

> All day long the children drive around in trucks and jeeps, with the soldiers on duty. And the soldiers off duty are to be seen striding around, proud youngsters hoisted to their shoulders, and a string of others trying in vain to keep in step. They love the children and the children worship them—even some of the big children!

Uncle Sam's characteristics are not avuncular, but fatherly—even to that very healthy and helpful attitude, that one is expected to stand on one's feet as soon as possible.

During these war years, although overburdened by responsibility and work, his representatives in the Department of State and the consulates met with courtesy every inquiry, and dispatched available information with a promptness that has been a just cause for admiration and appreciation.

At the repeated request from the people, who finally made formal application to the Archbishop, three Sisters on April 17, 1945, went back to Malabon.

By April 19th all the other Sisters were at Santo Tomas living in tents, and looking for a house sufficiently intact in which they might make a new start in the once beautiful city, now marred by shell, wantonly gutted by fire, with familiar landmarks missing or but specter shafts against the tropical sky—as the dome of the Cathedral, the spires of Santo Domingo, of San Ignacio! Filipino friends, out of their gracious charity, offered homes to the Sisters for school and conventual purposes. These were accepted gratefully. On May 2nd, Sister Trinita writes to Mother Mary Joseph:

We have permission to make any changes we need. There will be many inconveniences—lack of space, water, light—as have marked all Maryknoll beginnings—but the past three years showed us how few things we really need! With fine faith in God's loving Providence, and confidence in the fidelity of the people, we start again—without worldly possessions except a five gallon tin, full of tin cans, all shapes and sizes, which we use for dishes.

When the Immaculate Conception Sisters heard we were sallying forth, they offered some of their school furniture—they have the furniture but no house!

By truck, on May 4th, a group returned to Lucena. Sister Maura Shaun describes briefly this trip:

Passing through the towns going south, we saw the work of destruction that marked the Japanese Army's passage and defeat. Santo Tomas, Batangas was very bad indeed. San Pablo (formerly the site of Baker's coconut plant) is a complete wreck and so is Tiaong. Other towns were partly destroyed. I think Sariaya and Lucena are the least damaged. The poor people are sticking to the ruins, living in shelters of burned tin and fresh bamboo and existing on almost nothing. We waved most of the way to Lucena—to little groups surprised and glad to see us.

At Lucena, the Sisters found the convent roof and walls intact but plumbing, hardware, fixtures and furniture gone. The house had been headquarters for the Japanese military police. The domestic science department they had lined with galvanized iron. The electric connections and other instruments spoke potently to Sister Trinita of their uses. The Sisters have once again taken over works of peace, if teaching belongs to that state of beatitude! After three and a half years of freedom from school, the younger generations are exposed to an educational system without benefit of book, bell, or blackboard. "In the beginning was the Word."

Maryknollers were back in the Mountain District before Baguio was taken by the Americans. They entered the town in the footsteps of the army of occupation. On the rent roof of the Convent, and in their free time, the soldiers did a temporary repair job. The concrete walls were eyelet-ed. But the typhoon season was moderate: "I think God looked down on our patched covering and tempered the elements!" writes Sister Constance. Most of the furniture was looted, the sewing machine included. Materials for clothing arrived from the Motherhouse, but when the community blossomed forth in new habits, they were sewed on a machine borrowed from the Igorotes.

Meanwhile activities extend from catechism instructions to catering. The extracts from the diary of a week read in part:

August 1, 1945: For the next few days we shall be busy running around with jeep and truck to find enough dishes, tables, linens, cooking utensils, for the wedding breakfast which Father Reilly has asked us to serve for two army officers, a Lieutenant and a Nurse, who are to be married August 6th at the Cathedral. As there is no place where the wedding party could have their reception, Father asked if we would take care of them here. However, five cups—and they include patterns from three prewar sets—will never provide formal service for forty guests, so we are forced to go hither and yon for everything except a house.

August 6th: The wedding day. The chef, the food, the pianist, the waiters, and the punch sergeant were a few of the early arrivals for the wedding breakfast preliminaries. We were fortunate in being able to get Benguet lilies, fragrant blossoms with lacy, fern-like leaves, similar to St. Joseph lilies, which grow in the woods here. Menu cards, each with an appropriate quotation from *Evangeline*, were made by the Belgian Sisters on sinamay, a native cloth woven from abaca fibre. The St. Paul de Chartres Sisters did their bit by dressing a miniature bride and groom. Guests included forty army officers, all of whom were profuse in their thanks for what they referred to as the first bit of home they have enjoyed since they joined the army.

"Santa ex machina," the 1945 Christmas variation for Malabon was enjoyed to greater or less extent according to age, responsibility and distance from the theater of action.

From midnight well on to noon, we were busy with the tender touching ceremonies of welcoming the Christ Child to His fire-tried earth. The breakfast table bore colored *stateside* apples, no less! In the early afternoon came Santa traditionally garbed, riding through the sky in a helicopter, successor to Donner and Blitzen. It was a partly charity, and a wholly commercial stunt. Gifts for the children were not subordinate to but dependent upon the demonstration staged to show the manoeuverability of the machine. Newsreel men and newspaper men were much in evidence until the mob scene began. The Sisters' part of the program was to provide the children which we did all too well. Even Santa in the personable person of Major Alfred E. Smith, Jr. quailed and begged a Sister to take over—"Here you give out this stuff! I'm going up!" But some of the G.I.'s got him atop a jeep whence he dispensed his largess. Burly M.P.'s mopped their brows and pleaded with the Sisters to establish order. We were successful only in comparison to the failure achieved by six M.P.'s, two colonels, three lieutenants, two majors, one captain and a couple of dozen assorted soldiers. Sister David Marie with military strategy divided the crowd—not by force of arms or imposition of will or any method proposed in education texts, but by becoming a distribution center for Wrigley's. She had foreseen an emergency and prepared accordingly.

The lighter moments are respites amidst tragedy. Sister Trinita was called to testify at the War Guilt Trials. On November 16, 1945, she writes:

On Wednesday I was summoned to appear as a witness in the Yamashita case. I was asked to describe conditions in the women's cell at Fort Santiago and to give a general picture of the guards and military police there after October 9, 1945, the date when Yamashita took command in Manila. The authorities have not been able to locate one other prisoner of that period! Only God knows why I am alive! . . .

The ballroom of the High Commissioner's house where the trial is being heard is crowded daily with G.I.'s, Navy, Nurses, Wacs, all eager for a sight of Yamashita. And with such an opportunity, in my excitement, I forgot to look at him.

At the same trial appeared Rosalinda, an eleven-year-old girl, whose parents were killed by the enemy, and she herself slashed by bayonets. Her story travelled across the world. A Manhattan gentleman who read the story over his cup of morning coffee arranged to adopt her. To assure her a Catholic name and Catholic education, he requested the Maryknoll Sisters to act as his proxy. The world of the missions is full of lost children. The Sisters tell of a brother and sister team:

When the First Cavalry (American) were fighting their way into Manila, they found Billy and immediately annexed him to their outfit. When they moved southeast to Lucena, they took Billy with them; and if they could have smuggled him into Japan when they went there in August, they would have done so. But as that was impossible, the next-best thing was to take him to our Sisters, who learned from him that he had a little sister.

From the information he gave, Sister Miriam Thomas was able to trace the nine-year-old girl to a house in Paco, where she was working as a little servant. Now both children are with our Sisters in Lucena and are going to school. G.I.'s taught Billy his English, and he is in Grade Four. Benny is in the first grade but will have to stay there a bit longer, as she does not know English.

* * * *

Sister Paul remained in Kunming, China, after V-J Day, which fell on the feast of Our Lady's Assumption, August 15th—until the missioners cleared for the South. The Sisters teaching in India remained until the end of the school year when they flew Mt. Everest and returned to their stations.

The condition of a once flourishing Mission is described by Sister Rose Victor:

Yes! here we are in Laipo, back among the ruins. You would

really need a few pictures of our place to visualize the extent of the damage and our present living quarters. Completely destroyed are the Church, Rectory and Probatorium. The convent is missing its two wings; the center, with a staircase well scorched, stands. It furnishes us with our present living quarters, houses the native Sisters, and all the transients! We walked down town—people are picking bricks from the debris with which to start rebuilding. The only familiar sight on this market day were the peddlers in evidence with racks of colored threads, buttons, old clothes, wooden shoes—salvaged from the wreck.

Sister Antonia Marie, M.D., did heroic service through a cholera epidemic in Kweilin and at a primitive hospital in Chaotung where a group of Maryknoll Sisters helped two Yugoslavic Sisters care for natives and minister to American soldiers. She waited and worked in Laipo until living quarters were available in her mission, for Kweilin was left a ghost city! A four-room brick building remained of the Sisters' compound. Sister became consultant to the Kweilin branch of U.N.R.R.A. Now she is "at home" in two dispensaries.

Throughout interior China roads are bad, pitted with shell holes, worn by tramping feet of marching armies and of fleeing civilians, rutted by heavy machines of war; bridges are bombed out, washed out, and replaced with narrow native ones of doubtful integrity, or not at all, which latter call for slipping down and scrambling up banks, and fording streams.

After a trip of this sort, Sister Moira and Sister Chanel found the convent at Taanchuk machine gunned, looted, without furniture, floors removed and window frames gone. Thence, a twelve mile hike to Pingnam, where the convent was better in that the floors were intact; but bloodstained! The native Sisters were on hand to give a welcome. They had returned recently from the hills where they sought safety, at one time in disguise. Work was started again. Everywhere the Christians are in evidence and are faithful.

In Kowloontong, the convent was intact but occupied by some thousand Japanese wounded. All large buildings on Hong Kong and on the mainland were commandeered for hospital purposes.

For months, in a small rented cottage, the Sisters lived and planned the future. As the school was slowly emptied, the Sisters moved in by way of the basement, where they had found shelter the first months of the war! In time, the whole but furnitureless house was again theirs. The situation of the British Colony as described in a diary of January 1946 was desperate:

Schools remain unsettled with parents begging admission for their children, with no teachers, with texts unavailable, with Code regulations tightening up to normal living conditions, despite the fact that living conditions do not approximate normalcy.

Food prices are mounting steadily; with increasing population —and border control of returning refugees is impossible—the food supply is unequal to the demand. Black markets, reportedly replenished from Allied ships in the Harbor, flourish! The people with money pay inflation prices for delicacies, while the poor pay for refuse—ends of bread, half-eaten sausages, scraps of fat—thrown overboard and salvaged by vendors. A new luxury for the poor is being able to buy a piece of bread toasted while one waits, and over which has passed a spot of pilfered jam!

From Seoul, Korea, a friend wrote on October 7, 1945:

Thanks to God the world peace has been restored and the long oppressed Korea has finally been liberated from the yoke of Japan! The great joy that the Koreans now experience is so thrilling that no word can express it properly. All this we owe to the heroic sacrifices of the American Forces and we can never forget this great indebtedness, and we feel that we must do our own part in trying to repay this debt in some way or other within the reach of our capacity. We also are very grateful for your constant prayers which brought this wonderful result.

The Catholic Church here in Seoul is brightened with a very promising future. The religious liberty is fully guaranteed and the Governor, General Arnold, is a Catholic. Also there are several thousand Catholic soldiers in the army who fill up the Cathedral every Sunday. We are quite proud now that we are Catholics.

The memorable Feast day of the Korean Martyrs was indeed a day of jubilation for we had a Solemn Thanksgiving Mass, celebrated by Bishop Ro to which General Arnold and thousands of officers and soldiers attended; and after Mass, we gave them a big, big reception for which they were very much pleased.

Sister Agneta and her Sisters are all well and safe. Needless to say she went through such a hardship during the long years of the war that we all feel that it was a miracle that she survived. One could write volumes to record all the agonies and trials she had to go through.

As you know, she is under the control of Russian forces—that is quite a different country. 38° is the dividing line.

Sister Agneta on October 14, 1945 wrote to Mother Mary Joseph. Through the kind offices of a chaplain, it reached Maryknoll some five months later!

Glory and Praise Be to God!

My Reverend and dear Mother:

Mother how I wish to talk to you directly instead of through this paper! I heard yesterday that a letter from America has come for me. I have not received it as yet, but hope to receive it soon. First of all, how are you, dear Mother, and all our dear Sisters, at home and abroad? During the last four years of trial I have never left you in spirit or rather the thought of your prayerful remembrances kept me going. It must have been very difficult for you all during the war. Here we suffered from all angles, physically, mentally and also materially. Besides the air raid, we lived in constant anxiety of being put out of this house, for many parties wanted to use it for their own purposes, and the fear of the possibility of the Sisters being called out for army service. Even on August 15th we spent from 2 to 4 A.M. in the underground hole, for air planes were flying over us. But three o'clock in the afternoon brought us the most happy news of the long-prayed-for peace. Yes, peace! and we leave it to your imagination how happy we all were. We believed peace really would reign and thought we were truly free. But! Now we are in a most strange situation indeed. Under the Soviet Military administration, we live in a constant terror, especially all women do.

On August 30th a truck drew near to our back door, and before we knew it five of the Russian soldiers were in the house going through every room. Not knowing the language, they made signs, guns and swords pointed to our chests. They were in the house about half an hour. None of us was hurt in any way. However the purpose of their visit was clearly seen, and in order to avoid the immediate danger, all of us, eighteen in number, left for Peng Yang in secular clothes. But even there it was not safe, and finally I had to send all the novices and postulants home, temporarily. And the professed sisters were dispersed among the Christian families. Those days of sorrow were indeed a trial to this infant community. In spite of all darkness, hoping against hope we prayed for God's assistance. At last through the kind efforts of friends we finally succeeded in obtaining some sort of document of protection from the headquarters, to be shown to any intruder. With a feeling of certain safety, gathering the Sisters together, all returned to our convent after a ten days' absence. That evening the *Te Deum* was sung in the chapel which we had left in many tears. Even after our return they came around every two or three days, and tried the doors of the house to see if they could gain entrance. The railroad station and the oil supply house being near here, many of them are stationed at Sopo. So we keep our doors closed and lights covered at night, for they are sure to come in when they see the light. People are being robbed of their clothes and money, women insulted, some killed. Every day we hear all sorts of cruel news—even as I am writing the sound of shooting is heard. Some days ago they broke into the Pyenyang Sisters' house, besides the Bishop's office.

As yet we have no newspaper, no distant telephone calls, no communication of letters. Our country has been divided, there is no way of going up to Seoul without walking 200 ri. and at that very risky, I am told. No one knows as to how and who divided it, nor how long this condition would continue.

For myself, I have been very well, except for three months during which I was confined to my bed. Am trying to carry on the work which is over and above my strength. I still am wearing the native Sisters' habit, except for the ring. And am saying the Office in Korean with the Sisters. Our native Sisters' community had been growing slowly. At present the entire community numbers thirty-two, of which twenty-one are professed, and are working in six different houses—Shingishu, Gishu, Anchu, Yeng You, Shrinri and Sangsukuri. There has been one death, that of our dear Columba, who came to us from Fushun in December, 1942, and went to her heavenly home the following November with T.B.

I would like to tell you many more things—in fact there is no end—but I must stop now, and hope God will grant me the opportunity of talking to you directly. I have not used English for so long, I am sure I have made many, many mistakes in this letter, and am sorry for you, for you will find difficulty in reading it.

At Mountain View, California, Mother Mary Joseph picked up the first word in three years of the Sisters in Dairen, Manchuria. She telegraphed the Motherhouse on September 7, 1945:

Army radio reports five Maryknoll Sisters rescued Dairen Well—clapped hands with joy on meeting American soldiers Sister Rose Ann among them. Without funds for a long time and no means of communication. Respectfully treated and allowed to carry on work.

A month later letters were received from the Sisters. The following excerpts are from a message written on September 13th by Sister Marie Elise. They tell something of the dangers and suffering to which the Sisters were exposed:

It has been a long, and sometimes very hard ordeal. But I am not complaining because it was all for the glory of God. The biggest strain, and the most disagreeable and dangerous time has been during these past few weeks, since the Russian Army has come in.

We tried to help the poor people who came running to us for protection, though we were not safe ourselves. Placing all our trust in the Sacred Heart and His Blessed Mother, we had them sleep in our convent, while we took turns on watch, day and night. Strain though it was, we laughed a lot after the scares were over, and so managed to keep quite sane. Many of the incidents were so terrible that I cannot write about them. . . .

Last night, the Feast of the Holy Name of Mary, we finally got word from Maryknoll's Bishop Lane.

As for the mission, there is ever so much work to do, and how we long for more Sisters to help do it! We think the future will be more profitable for God, though not easy. If, after all this, we can help more souls to get to heaven, we can happily say it was all well worth it, and not half bad.

I could go on and on, but as there are many sick to be cared for—doctors are very scarce—I must run along to do my share. We have felt your prayers and are so grateful for them, but please pray still more for us that we may carry on for the glory of God, His Blessed Mother, and Maryknoll."

His Excellency, Bishop Raymond Lane, released from concentration proceeded to Fushun, his episcopal city, thence he went to Dairen to see the Sisters. In a letter to Bishop James E. Walsh, Superior General of the Maryknoll Fathers, dated February 18, 1946, he pays tribute to the steadfastness of the Sisters:

If there has been anything approaching the heroic by Maryknollers in these parts, it is the conduct of our Maryknoll Sisters here in Dairen during these recent years—despite physical and mental sufferings, lack of food, etc. Their school is the result of their spirit of loyalty and perseverance. It now numbers almost two hundred students, and they could take twice that number if they had the personnel.

However, they are all in need of a rest and are only holding on until substitutes can come. Sister Sabina has done wonders and is the talk of the town for her work among the refugees. By the way, our little native Sisters in Fushun have been exposing their lives daily for the Japanese refugees, about two-thirds of whom have died there from typhoid, typhus, and dysentery, etc. Three of our Sisters have had typhus, two very nearly died. Our best Japanese catechist did. Three of our lay workers have had it. All of these people have been going to the refugee camps with food and medicine. We have had about a thousand baptisms in Fushun alone among the Japanese refugees.

An epic poem could be written about the work, the sacrifices, the suffering and the loyalty of both our Maryknoll and native Sisters during the years of the war. I wish you could see the habits of our native Sisters and the shoes of the Maryknoll Sisters. One gives away what one can to cover the naked. I am going to save a few relics of my own just to bring back and to show what Sisters can do to keep a garment from falling off one's back.

Regular communications or transportation—with 1946 half over—have not been established.

* * * *

In Hawaii numberless members of the armed forces found their paradise in the unofficial U.S.O. houses of the Sisters. Living for long years under the strain of blackout, threat of invasion, and overwork due to the difficulty of transportation of personnel from the States, the Sisters in Hawaii have listened to, fed, provided recreation for "our sisters and cousins, our uncles and our aunts," not forgetting fathers and nephews who go the

South Pacific way, in the various services for men and women in a warring world. One visitor returned with a few more. A censor, not a Catholic, asked a buddy of the Faith to take him to the Sisters—"I read in every letter something about their kindness; why do I have to learn it second-hand?" He didn't.

Sister Daniel, on Maui, describes the extra-conventual activities there:

The service men call our orphanage the U.S.O. On our Island, so far away from Honolulu, there is no Catholic center available to the men, so we try to make them feel at home. Our school library has been turned into a reading room for them. To add a touch of home, we try to keep cake and candy on hand, the good women of the parish furnishing the ingredients.

On Sunday mornings we serve breakfast to all the service men who receive Holy Communion, the parishioners supplying the food. The Sisters prepare it and the older boys get a real thrill out of helping to serve Uncle Sam's men.

The highest army officer on this Island, who is a daily communicant, comes to early Mass at our church each morning, Missal in hand, and afterwards has breakfast at the orphanage. Another high ranking officer is likewise a daily communicant, while the highest naval officer is a frequent communicant.

On the last Holy Name Communion Sunday here, five hundred service men received in a body with the local Holy Name Society and had breakfast with them afterwards in the school hall. The entire middle section of the church was filled with service men only.

The number of service men receiving Holy Communion at our Church increases each Sunday. Similar reports come from other parts of Hawaii. One pastor relates that the example of the service men has had a salutary effect upon the men of the parish. There is thus a beautiful giving and receiving, while the Church in Hawaii plays host to the Army, Navy and Marines.

Sister Marilyn's story of the first war Christmas was the same, with variations in 1942, 1943, 1944:

On the eve, one of the hundreds of soldiers who visit us every Sunday after Mass for coffee and doughnuts volunteered to be Santa Claus. He is a nice, stout fatherly soul who fitted the part perfectly. He dressed in our Santa Claus suit and sat under the big Christmas tree which was well lit with all sorts of electric light. Of course we planned this before blackout at six. I wish you could have been here to have seen the expressions on the little girls' and boys' faces when Santa handed them their presents. Some had never seen a tree before and never heard of a Santa Claus. Many had never had a doll before so we were compensated for our long hours of work in preparation for this surprise for the children, by the smiles that came over their little faces.

On Christmas the Captain of the Air Base invited the children to the field for the day! A bus came for them after Mass and away they went singing Christmas carols. When they arrived at the Base a child was put into the hands of a sailor whose duty it was to see that his child was taken to dinner, to a movie which was shown for the children's benefit, and to see Santa Claus. The jolly old fellow has gone modern! Much to the children's delight, he arrived by airplane. The machine made a beautiful landing and out climbed Santa Claus. Each child received a suit of clothes or a dress and a handsome toy beside. And not only was Santa Claus generous, but the sailors in charge of the children. Many one-dollar bills were handed in when they came home, to be kept for them to spend later for movies and whatever they wanted. So Christmas night found many sleepy but happy children.

We Sisters hardly knew where to begin to thank the Army and Navy for all they did to make the children happy. The Quartermasters spent almost all their free time in decorating the children's dining room. It is really beautiful. Any church would be glad to have the Crib they set up. If the Christ Child had come to Hawaii, it is exactly what He would have found!

Mother Mary Joseph visiting the Islands in 1945 noted many differences since the day in 1940 when she had watched with deep pride and supreme confidence the United States Fleet sail into the turquoise blue Hawaiian waters. She writes of Pearl Harbor which she saw with Father Slavin, Chaplain:

I recalled the section as I saw it in 1940, just a spot in the country to a casual observer, with a very second rate narrow road leading to it. Now it is the center, the heart, of a great military area, with fine four-lane roads, and every foot of land covered with tents, barracks, Quonset huts, drill grounds, recreation centers, Quartermaster's supplies. A lovely thing in the midst of all the materialism was Father Slavin's Chapel—a Quonset hut, transformed by the loving artistry and ingenuity of Catholic boys into a house of prayer. The walls were latticed letting in air and light. At the entrance were beautifully designed groups, in colors, of the Hawaiian flowers. The altar is of fine koa wood; instead of a dossal there is a beautiful bamboo backing; the stations, in color, are jig-sawed.

Father Hugues, chaplain on the Carrier *Enterprise,* when the Japanese struck, also acted as guide:

He called for us at Waikiki and drove us to the cemetery where the December 7th victims are buried, a sad, sad spectacle. Then we went into Pearl Harbor where Father reconstructed the whole tragedy for us. It was a rare experience. We drove through Hickam Field which I had seen in all its beauty and newness in the Spring of '41, under Father Sliney's guidance.

There is little beauty left there now.
On Maui—

Father Lustig, one of the chaplains, arranged for all of us to have an Amtrack ride and it was great fun even though we got well bounced about and soaking wet. You will recall that these were used when rescuing our Sisters from Los Baños in the P.I. On the morning of our last day, Major de Gugilielmo took us on a Carrier, a novel and most interesting experience. I have many interesting souvenirs to show you and many stories to tell of what our boys went through.
There was a departure dinner at the Home for eleven or twelve Chaplains who are leaving for the States.

All the men of the services, regardless of rank, show a deep spirit of gratitude for whatever is done for them. Mother thus describes her reception at the Children's Home in Wailuku, Maui:

We arrived at the Home to find Marines lined up on either side of the stone path, and as I passed between them to the house they gave me a great military salute. I really felt embarrassed, though touched and honored by the graciousness of these boys who have been at the Home and Convent long enough to have earned the title, "Maryknoll Marines."

They are a fine group of young men, generous, devoted, thoughtful, clean-living, fun-loving and courteous. I could not begin to tell you what they have done in the way of plumbing, painting and carpentry in their free time. They on their side feel they are the debtors to the Sisters for sympathy, prayers, advice and good meals and lunches plus pleasant social times and religious opportunities.

They were lovely to me—quite like my own sons—and I have told them that whatever Maryknoll Convent they visit will welcome them, and not let them go away hungry. So, please Sisters, welcome cordially any of these boys who may call on you. In other houses the Army, the Navy and the Sea Bees have been as helpful as they could and you will welcome them too, I know. I look forward to meeting them at Maryknoll.

After greetings were over, questions asked and answered and the children seen, Father Vaughan gave Benediction at which the Marine Choir, under Captain Warnescz, sang, even the *Te Deum* at the end.

Then we all sat down to a delicious dinner, while the Marines looked after the children. Some of them remarked that the Iwo Jima battle was easy compared with the conquest of these little folks who can devise a hundred ways to torment and tease their disciplinarians.

When we had finished our dinner, washed the dishes and reset the tables, the Marines were relieved of their unusual duty and solaced with a turkey dinner, too.

These boys are a living tribute to the teaching orders of the Church in America.

Maryknoll sees a spiritual meaning in her daughters' sharing of doughnuts with the men of the Services in Hawaii, and the soldiers' breaking of their C-rations with her children at far off Los Baños in the Philippines—*noblesse oblige!*

If the cessation of war brought more quickly a greater degree of peace to Hawaii than to other mission lands, there were trials of unexpected nature.

A Convent diary lists April 1, 1946 as

never-to-be-forgotten day for people living in Hawaii. Early in the morning rumors spread that there had been a tidal wave and that two new islands had been heaved up out of the sea off Waikiki Beach. Nearly everyone not on the shore took these reports as an April fool stunt. Then we had a phone call which dispelled our placidity. It was from Laniki where we had a rest house for the Sisters—or more exactly where one had been—for the message was to the effect that a tidal wave had practically destroyed our beloved St. Joseph's Convent by the sea, and that the five Sisters there had been in grave danger. Here is the composite story of the Sisters:

The Sisters were closing up early as they were due at their various posts in Honolulu to begin a working day. At about ten minutes to seven some one observed the unusual actions of the bay. The water receded far out beyond the coral reefs, then rushed in wildly. Twice the waves came up over the lawn beyond anything ever seen at the highest tide. The Sisters remarked the absence of wind, and proceeded to move lawn benches and chairs nearer the house. Inside, Sister Callista tuned in on the radio only to get musical programs. Then the Sisters on the lawn saw coming at a terrific speed what looked like a mountain of water. It was a tidal wave later estimated as ten feet high and moving at a rate of five hundred miles an hour. Sister Agnese had taken to the garage, started the car, with the intention of taking the Sisters to higher ground—but in a moment the motor stalled. Meantime the other Sisters rushed for the house—all made it except Sister Patrice, who was swept against a closed door—then as it broke, she fell into the living room. Fortunately she managed to keep her head above the water, and holding to a table draw herself to her feet.

Waist deep in water, the Sisters stood, in the midst of chaos. The force of the water shattered the window and doors on the front, forced in a large plate glass window and ocean-side wall of the living room and bedroom, then pushed out the roadside wall, sweeping the furniture out on the road two hundred feet distant. The chapel escaped. The Sisters somehow reached the road and were invited by signal to take safety at the home of Mr. Pope, reached by a climb of one hundred steps.

At a moment's notice all the Charities of Honolulu placed themselves at the disposal of the Red Cross. The Sisters will be forever grateful to Father Alphonsus who spent days in recovering the household goods of the Convent. Sister Jolenta of St. Francis Hospital dispatched a truck to move the salvaged furnishings to Honolulu. Mrs. McCullum, the Superintendent of the Kawailoa, sent four men and four girls to give aid. Mr. Lex and many other neighbors whose homes had been above the sweep of water gave aid. Our friends of the Services helped take over.

By the end of the day it was estimated that probably two thousand people were homeless on Oahu alone. The Army rose quickly to the occasion. Colonel Saffron in charge of the Jungle Training Center, obtained permission to evacuate Army personnel and to act as refugee center. The Army immediately transferred doctors and nurses to the camp to care for the evacuees.

We give thanks once again for the personal safety of the Maryknoll family.

* * * *

On February 13, 1945, Mother Mary Joseph gave the Community meditation. It was the eve of the twenty-fifth anniversary of the canonical establishment of the Maryknoll Sisters. The text of the meditation was

> UNLESS THE LORD BUILD THE HOUSE, THEY LABOUR IN VAIN THAT BUILD IT. UNLESS THE LORD KEEP THE CITY, HE WATCHETH IN VAIN THAT KEEPETH IT.
>
> Ps. CXXVI—1, 2.

A quick view of the peoples of the world aflame with hate; a brief glance at her community, tried and proved true in the furnace of war, but with much of its works destroyed; and then Mother reviewed the guiding principles laid down by Maryknoll's beloved Father, Reverend James Anthony Walsh—simple, sane, and spiritual—upon which the Congregation was founded:

Try to get the other's view.

Find and admit what is good in any proposition before objecting.

Politeness is not enough among Christians. It should be only the outward expression of tender solicitude and love in and for Christ.

A place for everything and everything in its place.

What is fit for the waste-basket and fire should not be found in one's work tray tomorrow.

Make a difference between feast and fast day fare.

Recall the high ideal expected of missioners.

These principles are worth studying. . . . They are the foundation stones of religious character on which God built our Society strongly, and which made us after years of trial and growth somewhat fit for acceptance by Holy Mother Church as an integral part of her religious family. . . .

He has blessed our efforts with growth. . . .

Our task on this anniversary day is unchanged. . . .

For the Sisters in war areas a silence of three years was broken by the receipt of this dauntless message.

* * * *

All civilians in the Philippines received the South Pacific service ribbon. Sister Colombiere and Sister Cornelia in Kunming were awarded the civilian decoration for distinguished service. They are rightfully proud of and grateful for their Country's honor. Mother Mary Joseph's accolade was recognition of the devotion to duty of each individual. She writes to the entire community—March 26, 1945:

The spirit of our Sisters under horror, terror, mental and physical strain, dire hunger, poverty and discomfort, has been a glorious evidence of their solidity and their confidence in and dependence on God—a great consolation to me. You will be proud of them as I am. . . .

* * * *

God in His Providence has watched over Maryknoll—her sons and daughters. And they, with the eyes of Faith have seen

. . . Christ walking on the water,
Not of Genesareth, but—

the lordly Hudson, the West River, Manila Bay, the vast Pacific.

Index